WHAT IF SOMEONE SEES US?

WHAT IF SOMEONE SEES US?

Creative Nonfiction by New Writers

Collected and Edited by Guy Allen and Divya Maharajh

Life Rattle Press Toronto, Canada

What If Someone Sees Us?
Creative Nonfiction by New Writers

Published in Canada by Life Rattle Press, Toronto

Copyright 2023 by the contributing authors

All rights reserved. The use of any part of this publication, reproduced, transmitted in any form, or stored in a retrieval system, without the prior consent of the author is an infringement of copyright law.

Library and Archives Canada Cataloguing in Publication

What if someone sees us?: creative nonfiction by new writers / collected and edited by Guy Allen and Divya Maharajh.
(New writers series)

ISBN 978-1-989861-61-5

1. Creative nonfiction, Canadian (English)--Ontario-- Toronto.

I. Allen, Guy, 1947-, editor of compilation
II. Maharajh, Divya, 1985-, editor of compilation
III. Series: Life Rattle new writers series

Edited by: Guy Allen and Divya Maharajh
Cover Design by Laurie Kallis
Cover Illustration by Lena Spoke
Typeset by Laurie Kallis

Contents

Preface..1

Chapter 1: The Child

Guilt..9
Sunny Ahn

Sesame Street 11
Laurel Waterman

Prayer..14
Mahsal Nihal

The Hair Appointment 17
Lara Abike

My Father's Voice.. 23
Mark Sidney Joseph Auger

A Secret 29
Huiqi Zeng

The Stovepipe Hole 33
Elizabeth Clark

Chapter 2: School

The Eurocentric View...41
Jay Stephen

Piss.. 45
Sara Middleton

Operation Thumb Drive... 49
Bilaal Mohamed

The Black Turban...53
A.R. Adam

Sunday Afternoon..57
Paul Maka

The Pantsing...59
Madeleine Brown

Miss Fitzgerald... 62
Ebi Agbeyegbe

Choke... 65
Christina Hunter

Lakeview Indian Day School 70
Marylou Ceccile Debassige

Chapter 3: Family

The Good Boy... 77
M.A. Najfi

Little Bird 81
Phoebe Chin

Grandfather.. 83
Simin Emadzadeh

The Door.. 86
Rahul Sethi

The Visit 90
Mark Bialy

Put a Hole in It, Won't You.. 94
Emily Davidson

Mariage d'Amour... 97
Shelley Guo

Chapter 4: Relationships

Behind the Bushes.. 103
Bilaal Mohamed

Yellow 106
Andrew Ihamaki

Sneaking Out 109
Juliver Ramirez

The Birthday...113
Samantha Ashenhurst

The Summer Afternoon 117
Kael Reid

Love Struck 122
Naomi Wilson

Call It Even 126
Sandali Vithanage

Fate 130
Nadia Mohammad

I Love You Too... 137
Daniella Medel-Lawrence

Jump... 140
Emily Bonilla Rojas

Chapter 5: People

The Morning.. 145
Tara Monfaredi

ESSE Lights 152
Hijin Baasandorj

Buried the Jewish Way 155
Natasha Segal

An Old Jamaican Man 161
Janéa Achioso

Bill and Mr. Ram 165
Selina Africaine

Diamond Heights.. 169
Rachel Smith

Chapter 6: Places

The Back Stairwell 177
Saamiyah Ali-Mohammed

Finding the Moon 181
Jonathan Waugh

One Morning in Singapore 184
Gabrielle Ong

Deep in Southern Alberta 188
Helen Sproule

Harmonica 192
Gauri Menon

The Elevator 196
Bayan Khatib

Door FiftyFive.. 200
Miguel DaSilva

Chapter 7: Work

Code Blue 207
Mia Ortega

Fishmonger 211
Halah Butt

The Roti Shop 214
Selina Africaine

Washroom 1 218
Eileen Chen

Chapter 8: The Interview

Memories... 223
Donald Fitzgerald

Victoria... 227
Kael Reid

The First Stop.. 232
Rachel Smith

Eva Wilkins 239
Sara Middleton

Alexandra: Bébé de Sucre.. 244
Meghna K. Parhar

Block 16 252
Leegun Kim

Acknowledgements... 259

Preface

This collection contains fifty-five short, nonfiction stories by fifty-one authors. Some of these authors have gone on to have their work published or presented in public readings.

Few had experience as writers before they developed these stories as assignments for an introductory course in creative nonfiction at the University of Toronto. We teach in the Professional Writing Program within the Institute of Communication, Culture, Information & Technology at the University of Toronto. We treat students as writers, and we teach them to think of themselves as writers.

Some features of our limited-entry program deserve mention. We limit classes to thirty-five students. Our introductory course, *Creative Nonfiction*, operates as a supportive and intensive prose boot camp. Instructors work as editors to recommend revisions to the writers in their course.

Our courses emphasize narrative instead of the expository "writing for academic purposes" taught in many university courses. Students often resent the academic paper's prescriptive, rule-bound restraints with its ties to colonial customs. New writers embrace narrative. Narrative allows them to feel like (and become) real writers. They think narrative matters. It tells their story. They work hard to get the craft right.

Preface

Narrative in the Classroom

Narrative feels natural to our students. They have studied stories for all their school lives. Why can they not write them? Why can they not write in the traditions of the world's best writers? Why can they not write in the traditions of their cultures? Why can they not use the language they live in, often too colloquial for academic discourse?

Ironically, we find that students who master narratives about their lives relax about writing and fit easily into the more formal attire of academic discourse. They have learned how to handle language instead of feeling that language handles them.

Like some other courses in the program, our introductory course uses a peer-model collection. A peer-model collection contains exemplary narratives written by former students of the same course. We aim to update the peer-model collection every decade. This collection, *What If Someone Sees Us: Creative Nonfiction by New Writers*, comes out nine years after its predecessor, *Showing the Story* (published in 2014). We have kept some of the best from the 2014 collection. We have added thirty-three new stories.

Narrative Writers Become Educators

The authors in this collection become educators through the power of narrative. The writers show readers things we have not seen before. They take us to other times and places. I offer three examples of lessons we learn from the stories in this collection.

"Lakeview Indian Day School" by Mary Louise Cecile Debassige teaches us about the experience of First Nations people in the mid-1970s—before most people knew about the evils of the government and church-run school system for First Nations students. "The

Eurocentric View," Jay Stephen's narrative written in the 1980s, describes what happened when he asked a teacher how "Columbus discovered the Caribbean when there were people already there." Jay teaches us about the miseducation promoted in the standard white colonial curriculum. "Fate" by Nadia Mohammad teaches us about the challenges of navigating romantic love in a culturally conservative Muslim household. We observe difficult situations people face and the impact their choices have on their lives.

The University of Toronto blesses its students and teachers by filling our classes with people from cultures around the world. Our students share their work and teach each other about the places they come from and the lives they lead. They teach their professors.

The Selection and Editing of this Collection

Divya Maharajh, Lecturer in the Institute of Communication, Culture, Information & Technology at the University of Toronto, Mississauga, worked closely with me, day-by-day and story-by-story to select and edit this collection. Divya, a talented editor and teacher, brings her head and her heart to the text. She knows the technical demands of editing, but, more importantly, she feels and works with the nuances that represent the soul of a story. I have edited many texts. Divya has set a new standard for collaborative editing.

Divya and I collected narratives from several *Creative Nonfiction* instructors. We talked about principles for selection. We wanted the stories to model the principles of craft we teach in our introductory classes. Over the past five years, we also noticed pronounced shifts in the subjects that students wrote about. One of those shifts, mental health, has become a prominent and explicit theme in our students' narratives. Another increasingly prominent theme, sexual

Preface

orientation, arose from many stories about love and relationships within LGBTQ+ communities. Divya and I reflected these shifts in the work we chose to include in this collection.

A Word on Peer-Model Texts

I published my first peer-model text, *No More Masterpieces: Short Prose by New Writers*, in 1989. It was scary and new, an unheard-of trespass into sacred academic territory. Publishers either wanted nothing to do with it, or they wanted to change it into something that looked more like standard first-year writing texts. Professor Jack Wayne at Canadian Scholars' Press recognized the project's value and helped me publish a book honouring student voices. He did not insist on the editorial clutter other publishers wanted to add to the text to give it academic legitimacy.

The text worked as I hoped it would. It inspired more excellent narratives by students who acted more like writers than students.

Peer-model texts power the writing classroom and send powerful messages to students:

1) Your professor esteems student writing;
2) Students like you, with your same preparation and circumstances, produced these narratives, and you can do that too;
3) Your professor takes your writing seriously and has brought to it the same editorial expertise and book design work that professional writers enjoy.

Given opportunity, guidance, support, and respect, many can create moving, sensitive, funny, shocking, sad, and informative writing. No good reason suggests why a select few should monopolize the

Preface

pleasure, power, and release of expressive writing. We hope this collection will stimulate others to write and to see themselves as writers.

Guy Allen
University of Toronto
January 2023

Chapter 1: The Child

Present a short, detailed account of an experience you had or observed as a child.

Guilt

Sunny Ahn

"So," Mom yells, "your little five-year-old brother is the one to blame?"

"No," I murmur.

"I'm taking one of you upstairs. Who will it be?"

I stand silent. Sungho, my little brother, cries. Mom grabs Sungho's wrist and drags him upstairs. I remain in the living room. "I'm gonna teach you a lesson," Mom tells Sungho. His soft cries turn into screams of fear.

I know Mom's weapon of choice—a long, blue Little Tikes golf stick.

I cry for Sungho. I cry softly. I don't want Mom to return.

Bam! A door slams.

Mom yells at Sungho. I run halfway up the stairs to listen. I do not want to get caught in front of the bedroom door.

Mom yells in Korean. Sungho screams.

"Hyung did!" he cries. Hyung means "older brother" in Korean.

"Well, Hyung said you did it. Give me your hand!"

I scrunch my face. I listen to the slaps on Sungho's tiny hand.

He screams. I'm a horrible brother, I think.

Jeehyun, my little sister, approaches me on the staircase. "Poor Sungho," she says.

"Yeah," I say.

Jeehyun squeezes her eyes shut with every slap. I cover my ears. We both keep our heads down.

Chapter 1: The Child

Sungho screams louder. He sounds desperate. The slapping goes on and on. Mom knows I'm listening.

I grab Jeehyun's hand and rush down the stairs. I turn on the television. *Sponge Bob Square Pants* plays. Tears run down Jeehyun's pink cheeks. The house goes quiet. Mom must be done.

The door opens. The hinges squeak.

Mom shuffles down the stairs and into the kitchen. She ignores us and sits at the kitchen table.

Silence.

I hide behind the wall and spy on Mom. She sits motionless. The sun shines on her face. She cries.

I run upstairs. Sungho lies on the bed. He sweats. Blankets, pillows and a plastic golf stick lie scattered on the floor. Closed curtains cover the windows.

"Hey, you okay?" I ask.

Silence.

I lie down next to Sungho. He puts his arms around me. I hug him.

"Hyung, I'm sorry," he says. Sungho is innocent. His apology hits me like a brick.

"Sorry for being a bad brother," I say. I hug him tighter.

Mom cries. Sungho cries. I cry.

Mom and I don't talk for a week. Sungho, I think, is a better brother than me.

I feel guilty.

I also feel glad I did not get beaten.

Sesame Street

Laurel Waterman

I don't want to stay in bed anymore. Though I hear no cars on Duplex Avenue, the sky lightens outside my bedroom window. I can't hear anything inside the house. I scramble my feet from under the sheet and slide down from my pink canopy bed onto the shaggy green rug. I feel crumbs with my bare feet as I walk the two steps from my bed to the door. The hinges squeak as I pull the door open.

The narrow hall to Daddy's room seems long and dark. I see only shapes. The wooden railing guides my trip to the end. Daddy's breathing gets louder. He snorts at the end of each breath, pauses, then starts a new one. I stand in the doorway. He looks different without his glasses—like someone else's daddy.

He's alone—no lady friend beside him this morning. I tiptoe to the side of the bed.

"Daddy," I say, "can I go downstairs and watch *Sesame Street*?"

"Umhmm."

Silence.

"Daddy?" I poke his hairy ear.

"What does the clock say?"

I read the red numbers off the clock radio beside his bed. "It says 6-4-7."

"When it says 7-0-0, it's time for *Sesame Street*," he mumbles.

Usually, he speaks slowly, in a loud, low voice. Now he whispers.

Hot air blows out of the metal floor vent beside his bed. I sit on the vent and make a tent over my knees with my faded pink night-

Chapter 1: The Child

gown, the one with a padded Raggedy Ann face on the front. I play with her red yarn braids and stare at the clock. I put a braid in my mouth and chew.

"Daddy, it changed to 6-4-8!"

"When it says 7-0-0, you can go downstairs and turn on the TV." Daddy scratches his nose and rubs his eyes. He doesn't open them. His big nostrils stretch when he breathes in. I can see up his nose. I don't have nostril hairs like his. He has dents on his nose where his glasses usually sit. He looks better with his glasses on.

"Daddy, how much longer until 7-0-0?"

No answer.

I curl up and fold my arms and face into the nightgown tent. The heat puffs my nightgown out. The warm air blows on my skin and feels nice. I play with my toes.

"Daddy, how much longer?"

"About ten minutes." He yawns without moving.

I stare at his face and his long bushy eyebrows. A few silver, wiry ones reach halfway up his forehead. I want to touch his bald spot. It's soft.

The warm air stops, and my puffed-out nightgown deflates. The heat seeps out. I get goosebumps.

"Daddy, you look better with your glasses on."

His eyes open halfway. He studies me for a second and smiles. "You're just used to seeing me with them on."

He flips the comforter back and sits on the edge of the bed. His feet look big at the bottom of his skinny, hairy ankles. A few strands of his grey hair stick straight out on the left side of his head.

He reaches for the nightstand, finds his glasses and puts them on. "Okay, sweetheart." Daddy holds out his hand. I take it, and he pulls me up. "Let's go downstairs."

I trail behind him down the hallway.

Daddy walks down the creaky stairs. "What do you think, pancakes or French toast for breakfast?"

I smile. "Blueberry pancakes."

"I think we can manage that."

I stop halfway, plop down the middle stair, and bum my way down the rest.

"Daddy?"

"Yes, sweetheart?"

"Is it time for *Sesame Street* yet?"

Prayer

Mahsal Nihal

My covers bury me. Maybe this won't be real if I hide from it. My blanket lies thick over my head but does little to soothe the burning ache in my heart.

I should've known he was drifting away.

There weren't a lot of signs, though. He usually keeps to himself.

Still, after five years, I should've known him better.

I know a lot about him. I know he has black hair like my own and honey-brown eyes. I know his favourite song is "Thriller" by Michael Jackson. I know he can't swim but loves to dance.

Though I still missed what was right before me, trivial facts litter my mind. Today, Zayn Malik left the boy band One Direction.

I struggle to wrap my head around it.

Why did he leave?

Wasn't he happy?

Were the past five years of the band a lie?

I don't have the answers. At the same time, I'm not sure I want to know. With all the might of a heartbroken eleven-year-old, I decide I'll never let myself love again.

"Mashal!" someone shouts from downstairs.

I ignore it. I'm going through a breakup right now. There's no other way to describe everything I'm feeling: betrayal, anger, crashing waves of sadness. My chest heaves as I breathe in and shudder weakly, staving off another meltdown.

No, I decide. This is worse than a breakup.

I hear footsteps over the music my CD player blasts, "Where Do Broken Hearts Go?" a track from the new One Direction album, *Four*.

Four, I think. Harry, Louis, Liam, Niall—not Zayn—that's four.

I want to cry again.

Knock knock.

"Mashal," Mama calls. "We're going to be late for prayer."

I don't move.

The door creaks open, and Mama yanks off my sheets. Mama glares. "Get up," she scolds, "You've cried enough."

My eyes clamp shut as I hold back another barrage of tears. Mom may be right. No boy could be worth this much weeping.

"I've prayed enough too. Zayn was special." My voice cracks. I flush in embarrassment. I try to wrestle my sheets from Mom's hands, so she won't see me cry.

With a rough hand wrapped around my arm, Mom yanks me out of bed. "Only God is special. The devil is making you feel this way."

Mom shuts my music off and pulls me down the stairs, where the rest of my siblings, Mayra, Danyal, and Maazia, silently wait. She throws my shoes at my feet. "Put them on."

"No!" I kick my feet. I'm angry. She's angry. Mayra ushers the younger siblings out the door. It's just us now.

I cross my arms and glare at Mama.

She crouches down to my height, tilting my tear-stained face to hers. "If you come to prayer, I'll ask the imam to pray for him to rejoin the band

I straighten up. It's too late to stop Zayn from leaving, but now that he has, maybe I can bring him back.

"Okay?" she asks.

Chapter 1: The Child

"Okay," I agree.

She hands me my shoes again. I put them on.

The Hair Appointment

Lara Abike

Dad left. He had travelled back to America a few months ago, leaving me, my baby brother, Redwan, and my mom behind in our two-bedroom apartment in Abeokuta, Nigeria.

Father took me to the barber shop when he still lived with us. I sat in his lap as his barber shaved my head. I listened to the conversations between my dad and his friends. But now my hair had grown past my earlobes. My mother thought it was time I started doing it like the other four-year-old girls in our neighbourhood. She wanted it to look like Titi's, my cousin's, with her long black braids and straightened hair.

Mother often sent me to play with Titi while she talked with Titi's mother. When my hair grew out after my father left, Titi was the first to notice. We sat in her living room next to the round mahogany table as our mothers sat on a white sofa.

Titi combed through her doll's blond hair. Her dark brown eyes traced the movements of her comb as she worked through the hair. "I wish I had hair like this," she said. I nodded. Titi smoothed her beige comb on her black button-up dress, removing pieces of yellow hair. "I feel bad for you, Lara."

My mother's head tilted towards Titi and me.

"You used to have no hair," Titi said. "And now that you do, it doesn't look nice."

"Oh," I said.

My mother looked down at me.

Chapter 1: The Child

A few days later, my mother told me I was going to get my hair done.

"Will it hurt?" I asked.

Mom shook her head as she pulled my white cotton nightgown onto me and drew me into her queen-sized bed. She lifted the red quilt over us.

"It won't hurt," she said.

I nodded, then collapsed into her. Redwan slept in his low crib.

The next day my mother dressed in a button-up, white-collar shirt and black wool pants. She pulled an old, grey sweater over my head and fished out some black shorts for me to wear. She left Redwan with Titi's mom. I walked behind her, dragged ahead by my wrist.

"Where are we going?"

"We're visiting a friend."

A teenage peddler came up to us. The girl balanced containers of rice, pies, and sausages on a large tray on her head. A dark brown bob rested below the tray. Her almond-shaped eyes narrowed in on my mother. Her mouth opened.

Before the peddler could speak, my mother said, "No." Mom stepped around her, and we continued our walk. I turned my head to look at the peddler girl. She watched my mother drag me away, her eyes grim, her full lips set in a thin line.

We reached a small shack at the edge of our neighbourhood, enclosed by wilderness. Outside, a woman stooped over a young girl, a bit older than me, who sat between her legs. The woman, around my mother's age, braided the young girl's hair with wrinkled fingers. On her back, the woman had strapped a bald baby with a green rapa.

The Hair Appointment

My mother dropped my hand and waved at the woman.

The woman turned to us and smiled. She stood up from her stool and talked to my mother. They spoke in hushed tones.

My mom looked down at me and pointed at the young girl with the braids. Lines of braids extended from the top of the girl's forehead to the nape of her neck. "She's not much older than you, and she isn't crying. I don't want to hear anything about you making a fuss while getting your hair done," my mother said.

I swallowed the lump in my throat.

"I'll be finished with her in a few hours," the woman said.

My mother wrapped her arms around me. My arms hung stiffly at my sides. Mom rubbed the top of my head. "Be good," she said. She turned, left, and faded from view.

The smile dropped off the woman's face. She went back to braiding the other girl's hair. I sat on her patchy front yard beside the girl. Tears trailed down the girl's cheeks. Whenever the girl tried to raise her head, the woman pushed her head down.

The girl shed one last tear when the hairdresser finished, and the girl broke into a triumphant smile. She handed the hairdresser some blue and brown bills. "Do you need change?" the woman said, scowling. The girl shook her head and turned to go. She walked and then sprinted.

The woman crooked her head toward me. She pointed at the orange dirt patch between her legs in front of her blue stool. I lowered myself. She detangled my hair with a large brown comb. "So much hair," she said. "So rough." The teeth of the comb snared in my hair and pulled on my tight coils. My eyes watered and reddened.

"First I'll do the relaxer, then the braid."

"My mother only wants you to braid my hair," I mumbled.

Chapter 1: The Child

"No, she told me to relax your hair," she announced. "Wait here." She stood up and went into her shack. The baby on her back bounced as she shuffled. She emerged with a blue box. "This is the relaxer I'll use for your hair."

She opened the box and pulled out a cylindrical bowl and a bottle of pink liquid. The bowl contained a white paste below a nylon seal. The woman pulled open the seal, twisted the cap off the bottle, poured the pink liquid into the paste, and swirled the mixture with a wooden spatula.

"Rice," a voice called. "Fresh rice."

The woman turned her head toward the road. The peddler girl, the same girl my mother and I saw, came our way. The woman put the bowl of light pink paste beside her. My stomach grumbled.

"Hello, Ma," the peddler girl said.

"How much for the rice?" the woman asked her.

"Thirty naira," the girl answered. She looked in her early teens.

"I'll give you ten naira for it," the woman said.

"Ma," the girl grumbled. "Please, at least twenty."

The woman shook her head. "Ten, or get off my property."

The girl nodded. She knelt, lifted the tray off her head, and laid it on the ground. She pulled the lid off a container. The musky scent of freshly cooked rice wafted into the air. My stomach rumbled. The girl used a wooden spoon to fill a clear plastic bowl with long brown grains of rice. She locked eyes with me as she scooped. She remembered me. The girl scooped more rice into the bowl. The bowl brimmed with thick grains of rice.

"I gave you extra. Enough for you and the girl." She looked down at me as she spoke.

The Hair Appointment

The hairdresser handed her a red bill. "Thank you. You can leave now."

The girl placed her tray on her head, straightened, and turned away from us. Her outline faded as she continued up the road and chanted. "Rice! Fresh rice!"

The woman parted my hair with her left hand and ate the rice with her right. She sectioned my hair into four buns and used the spatula to scoop the pinkish paste out of the relaxer container. The fresh smell of rice mingled with the sulfuric scent of the paste. Despite the awful smell, my stomach still grumbled. I waited for the woman to offer me rice.

She finished slathering all four sections of my hair with the relaxer. Her right hand lowered the bowl to the floor.

I stared at the empty bowl.

"Okay, now we wait for your hair to relax. Tell me when it starts to burn."

"It's burning," I said.

"No," the woman said. "You need to wait longer."

The heat intensified. Ten minutes passed.

"It's burning," I said.

She ignored me and went back into her shack. Thirty minutes later, she came out. She no longer carried the baby on her back. My scalp felt on fire. I needed to scratch it.

I lifted my hand to my scalp and dug my blunt fingernails into it. I scratched through my hair, dragging my nails against the skin. The burning spread like a forest fire. I pulled my fingers away. Drops of blood dripped from my fingernails. Wetness crept down my neck. The pinkish paste on my hand had turned crimson.

Chapter 1: The Child

A strangled noise came from the woman's mouth. "What did you do?" she screamed.

"My head is burning!" I yelled back at her.

She wrapped her hand around my wrist, and dragged me into her dimly lit shack. I couldn't see in the tiny space. The burning on my head raged. The woman yanked me into a closet-sized room. She made me sit on a chair and lowered my head into a sink. Light shining in through the gaps in the roof showed trails of blood that stopped at my feet.

The woman turned on a tap and splashed my hair with water. The fire on my head raged. The ceiling blurred. The figure of the woman blurred. She spoke. I bit down on the inside of my cheek and drew blood. I rolled my head from side to side. The woman screamed. I couldn't hear her words. My head bled. My shoulders tensed. I closed my eyes.

I woke in my mother's bed, bandages around and my head. My mother and grandmother stood above me.

"You shouldn't have sent her to that woman," Grandma said.

"Titi's mom recommended her," Mom said. "I had no idea this would happen."

I remembered my mother refusing to tell me where we were going and I remembered her conversation with the woman and the hushed tones they'd used and I remembered the woman telling me my mother wanted me to get a relaxer.

"I had no idea this would happen," Mom said.

"You didn't tell her to do Lara's hair like that?" Grandma asked.

I gazed up at my mother from the bed.

"No, I only wanted the braids. She's too young for a relaxer."

My Father's Voice

Mark Sidney Joseph Auger

My former friend Stu yaps away in the seat in front of me. "Mark . . . why, oh why, Mark . . . did you skip class yesterday, Mark?"

Under the blackboard, our English teacher, Ms. Pazdior, sits at her desk and pencils something into her agenda. She doesn't look up.

Stu continues. "Hey, Mark!" Stu booms. He projects his voice to Pazdior's desk. "Mark . . . oh, why Mark . . . did you skip English yesterday?" He enunciates each word clearly and carefully. He chuckles to himself.

I try to read *Summer of My German Soldier*. I could easily lift my hand and thwack the back of his head.

"Ms. Pazdior won't like that you skipped, Mark."

I can't believe I told this goofball.

Ms. Pazdior flicks her head up at the mention of her name. She stands and walks towards us.

"What's this?" she whispers. "What did you say, Stuart?"

"Oh, nothing, Ms. Pazdior." He whispers now. "Sorry. I didn't mean for you to hear that."

She looks at me and then back to him. "Did you say Mark skipped yesterday?"

Stu shrugs and goes back to reading his book.

I look up from mine.

"Is this true, Mark?"

I open my mouth. I don't speak.

Chapter 1: The Child

Ms. Pazdior studies my face. We hold eye contact. Her eyebrows scrunch.

She spins around and marches back to her desk. She turns her agenda around and examines it. "Yes, yes," she mumbles to herself. She looks towards me. "Mark, do you mind if I speak to you . . . um . . . out in the hallway for a moment?"

"Ah . . ." I set down my book. "Yes, of course, Ms. Pazdior."

I stand up and follow her out. I glance down at Stu as I pass. His eyes stare at his book. A smile stretches across his cheeky face.

In the hallway, I close the door behind me.

Pazdior jumps into it. "Did you skip my class yesterday, Mark?"

Again, I look her in the eyes. I can't say yes. I can't say no. I breathe in. I look at her sagging cheeks, at her greying hair, at the oversized glasses on her face.

"Okay. I'll take that as a yes." She squeezes her lips together and places her hands on her hips. Her mom jeans rest high on them. "I just want you to know that I'll be calling your house tonight to tell your parents about this."

My eyes close, my brain deflates, and my stomach boils.

"Sure. Okay," I manage.

As soon as I walk into the house, the phone's in my hand.

"You going to call somebody or what?" my dad asks after five minutes of this.

"No, no. No, no." I set the phone back in its cradle. I smile at him with no teeth. I stake out a spot in the kitchen. My dad heads upstairs.

The phone rings. I whip it up to my face.

"Hello?" I grumble.

"Hi, Mark."

It's my mom.

"I'm just calling to say I'll be home a little late tonight. Do you mind telling Dad?

"How was school today?"

"Alright. Same old."

I hang up and creep into the dining room. I perch myself on a chair, stare at the china in the cabinet, and set the phone on the table beside me. My hand shakes.

My dad watches TV in the bedroom upstairs. The sound of baseball highlights echo down the landing. From downstairs, I hear cartoony boings and cha-chings. My brother must be in the basement.

I slink down the stairs and sit at the computer. I want to vomit. My younger brother, Paul, reclines on the couch and plays Sonic the Hedgehog on Sega Genesis. I want to join him. I sit so straight my back doesn't touch the chair. I plant my feet into the worn carpet like at the beginning of a sprint. I tear some tissues out of the box.

The phone rings. I fling it up.

"Hello?" I grumble.

"Hi, yes, hi. I'm looking for Mr. Auger?"

I cover the mouthpiece with tissue. I drop my voice an octave and scrape out the words, "Yes. Speaking."

"Mr. Auger?"

"Yes," I grate out.

My brother gapes at me from the couch.

"This is Ms. Pazdior, um, Mark's Grade 10 English teacher."

"Oh yes? Yes, yes. How can I help you?"

My brother pauses Sonic.

Chapter 1: The Child

"Um . . . excuse me . . . is this Mr. Auger?"

"Yes."

"Okay. Well . . . Mr. Auger . . . today it came to my attention that your son Mark skipped my class yesterday."

"Oh dear," I rasp. I feel bile in the back of my throat. I squeeze my eyes shut and pull the hoodie over my head. My world focuses on the mouthpiece of the phone. "That's not good." I muffle each word.

Ms. Pazdior continues. "I agree. This is certainly not. This is disappointing and completely unacceptable. I would like for him to serve a detention."

I nod my head. "Of course. He needs it."

"Do you know why he skipped?"

"Um . . . well . . . he has been a bit down recently. He loves the class, but he's been a bit down. I'll talk to him. He needs a talking to."

I need some water.

The pause hangs.

"Okay, great. Well . . . thank you . . . um . . . for discussing this with me, Mr. Auger. That's all I wanted to talk to you about. Have a good night."

"Good night."

I click end and crumple the tissues into my fist. I lean back in the chair and feel like passing out. The adrenaline keeps me afloat. My heart slows. I remove my head from the hoodie.

"You're in so much trouble," my brother says from the couch.

I glance over at him, pull out my wallet and slide a twenty-dollar bill across the table. I take a deep breath. He pockets the bill and unpauses Sonic.

I slouch and stare at the wall. My legs feel like mashed potatoes.

I manage a smile.

Then, I hear the steps.

Each stair pounds as my father descends from the top floor. My pulse trembles again. I watch the basement ceiling vibrate with each step. Stomp. Stomp. Stomp. He takes his time. His feet lurch onto the main floor as he loops to the top of the basement stairs. Quiet. From where he stands, I know he can see me. He's found me. His muffled steps descend the carpeted stairs behind me.

I pull my hood back up.

"Who was on the phone?"

My brother pauses the game again.

"Um. The phone?"

"Yeah. The phone." He enunciates each word clearly and carefully. "Who was it?"

"Um. Just a wrong number." I glance back at him and make brief eye contact. He stands on the bottom step. His gaze spews flame. I flinch away.

"Really?" he spits out. "Because when it rang, I picked up the extension in the bedroom. A woman asked for Mr. Auger. I opened my mouth to speak, but then . . . someone else did."

I pull my arms inside the hoodie.

"This other person had a nice, scratchy chat with this Ms. Pazdior."

His words slam through the cotton fleece of my hoodie.

"Just what the hell is going on, Mark?"

He waits.

"Now I know why you've been carrying that phone around like a damn baby." He swallows a rock. His words hammer down. "I'll tell you what will happen. Tomorrow . . . tomorrow, you will go into your English class. You're going to tell Ms. Pazdior, your English

Chapter 1: The Child

teacher, that she didn't speak with me tonight. She spoke with you. Yes, that's right. Then, you will apologize to her. After that, you will beg her to call here tomorrow night. I will speak to her then. Me. Not you. Do you understand?"

"Uh-huh."

"What's that?"

"Yes. I understand."

I need water.

"Then, when you get back home, you're grounded for the month. No Sega. No TV. No books. No friends. You can use the time to think over what you've done. Skipping class. Pretending to be me. You didn't even sound like me!" He sucks a lungful of air through his nose. "Is there anything else I should know about?"

I glance over at Paul on the couch. He holds the controller in his hands, his face pale and frozen.

"That's it," I mumble.

"Okay." He lumbers back up the stairs and into the kitchen.

I shake my head at myself. That voice. How could I ever think I could replicate that voice?

Eventually, I emerge from my hoodie.

My brother sets the controller down, stands up, walks over to me and pauses. He gently places the twenty-dollar bill on the table beside me and returns to his video game.

A Secret

Huiqi Zeng

Fifteen little sheep. Sixteen little sheep. Seventeen little sheep.

I squeeze my closed eyes even tighter. My fingers clutch a side seam of my pants. The soles of my feet sweat under my Hello Kitty blanket.

Through slits between my closed eyelids, I glance at the clock on the wall. The shorter needle points to the number one. The bell won't ring until it points at two.

The nap room, with all windows curtained, feels dull. Thirty-six kids sleep on two massive wooden platforms that lie alongside each other. A narrow aisle runs between the two platforms. Children place their pillows towards the aisle and their feet against the wall. The girl next to me sleeps soundly. The "Yulyu Kindergarten" patch sewn on her chest pocket rises and falls.

I turn around. I close my eyes again.

Forty-one little sheep. Forty-two. Forty-four. Forty . . . forty . . . where was I?

I peek at the clock again. The shorter needle still points at one. The clock must be broken.

It's bad enough to have a broken clock. But it's even worse to have Ms. Zeng on duty today. I scan the room and try to locate her. Ah, there she is. She sits cross-legged on a squeaky wooden chair near the door and watches all thirty-six of us.

Although we share the same surname, Ms. Zeng and I are not related. All of my uncles and aunts are short and chubby. Ms. Zeng

Chapter 1: The Child

is tall and slim. Her skinny hands, like two giant pale spiders, sit on her lap. Every time she smiles, her upper teeth stick out. She rarely smiles. She usually wears a pair of silver eyeglasses with thin stems, but she does not wear them now.

Ms. Zeng is the teacher in charge of discipline in our kindergarten. Whenever we have classes or playtime, she strolls around the classroom. She holds a long stainless-steel ruler behind her back and tap-taps on students' shoulders when they misbehave.

Tap-tap! "Line up quietly!" she yells in the corridor.

Tap-tap! "No leftovers! Finish your lunch!" She stands behind our dining table.

Tap-tap! "No chatting in class! Focus!" She frowns at the noise from the corner.

Tap-tap! "Go to sleep! And keep quiet!" she hisses between the platforms.

A "tap-tap" doesn't hurt. But it's scary. It comes from behind. You never know when you will get one. Ms. Zeng never misses. Nothing escapes her. My shoulders stiffen when I see her metal ruler.

Today, Ms. Zeng doesn't have the ruler. Nor does she take her usual stroll around the room. She sits silently for a long while.

She crouches over her knees and clutches her forehead with her hand. The old wooden chair lets out a quiet squeak. Several drops of water drip on her lap. A few seconds later, more drops rain down on her blue jeans.

Is she crying?

A light breeze through an open window ruffles the curtains and lets a shaft of sunlight into the room. The light shines on Ms. Zeng's head, turning a stray lock of her hair blonde. The blonde hair shivers every time she sniffs.

Ms. Zeng's thin shoulders shake. She presses both her hands over her mouth and tries not to leak any sound. She sobs silently. Her eyebrows twist with grief. A teardrop on her lap sparkles under the sunlight.

She *is* crying.

I remember this morning. Ms. Zeng stood at the front gate and greeted every student. When my mom kissed me goodbye, Ms. Zeng gave us one of her rare grins. "How lovely," she said to my mom and me but then looked away. I didn't know why she said that.

As my eyes move back to her, Ms. Zeng raises her head. Our eyes meet across the room. She looks stunned for a second.

The old chair squeaks again as Ms. Zeng leaves her seat. I hide under the blanket. I close my eyes, listen to my beating heart, and wait for a furious tap-tap.

Nothing happens. Ms. Zeng carefully sits on the step in front of my platform. Her hand pats my shoulder. "Can't sleep?" she whispers near my ears. Her voice sounds hoarse.

My body freezes.

"Did I scare you?" She smiles lightly. "Sorry," she sighs, "but can you keep a secret for me, please?"

I nod my head under the blanket and pull it off my face.

"Thank you." Ms. Zeng tucks me in and strokes my hair slowly, like a loving mother.

"Get some sleep now, little one." She rests her head on her elbow beside my pillow. Her hair touches mine. "You're gonna have a busy afternoon. And your mommy will wait for you at the front gate. She will give you a warm hug and a big kiss."

Chapter 1: The Child

Ms. Zeng sounds like she has something in her throat.

"So get some sleep now, little Huiqi." Her voice gets slower and slower, lighter and lighter. "Everything will be alright when you wake up. Sleep now."

Tears well in my eyes. I don't know why.

The Stovepipe Hole

Elizabeth Clark

I stand on a chair and wash the supper dishes. My nine-year-old sister Mary drys. The kitchen window reflects my ten-year-old face.

I shiver at the draft coming through a crack in the upper half of the window. The window looks over the snow-covered cornfield behind the farmhouse in the daytime. At night, the bare light bulb hanging over the big wooden kitchen table makes the window a mirror.

A long red gash marks my left cheek. Mary's right eye swells shut.

Dad sits behind us at the end of the kitchen table, surrounded by empty Molson Golden beer bottles. A butt-filled ashtray sits next to his elbow, and an empty pack of Player's Plain lies on the floor between his feet. Half-eaten spaghetti, pushed aside at supper, forms a hard crust on the plate near his other elbow. He jams his hands under his chin to keep himself from pitching forward into the mess on the table. The air, thick with cigarette smoke and the scents of beer, barn and spaghetti, upsets my stomach.

Katie and Lisa, the two youngest, eight and six, huddle together on the tattered, red sofa on the other side of the room under the big picture window that looks over the three barns at the bottom of the hill. The lights from the Warkworth Prison on the other side of the dirt road cast an orange halo in the sky. The halo stretches from Campbell's farm on one side of us to our grandfather's farm on the other.

Chapter 1: The Child

Mom works late at the nursing home as an aide on Saturday nights. She won't be home till after midnight.

Dad bolts up from the chair. He holds the edge of the table for balance.

My body jolts. I watch him in the window reflection. Lisa and Katie huddle tighter. Mary dries the dish in her hand over and over and looks straight ahead.

Dad walks silently toward the living room, holding his body rigid, forcing himself to walk straight. He ricochets off one side of the door jamb, then off the other side, and staggers into the semi-darkness of the living room.

Through the curtainless window in the living room, I see across the long, snowy pasture to my grandfather's brightly lit farmhouse. Curses follow a thud as Dad stubs his toe on a chair. He bounces off the cellar door into the middle of the room. He staggers backwards, bangs into the door leading to the upstairs, and staggers back into the middle of the room again. He reels forward and hits the half-open door of his bedroom. The door closes with a bang behind him. Springs squeak and groan as Dad flops down onto the bed. My sisters and I exchange silent glances. We look toward the back porch door at the other end of the kitchen. Above the back porch is our fourteen-year-old brother Sam's room.

Ten minutes pass silently while we wait to be sure Dad sleeps.

Loud snoring signals safety. I switch on the porch light and step under the round hole in the ceiling where the stovepipe used to go through to heat the upstairs. The two wood stoves are gone, replaced by the oil furnace, but Dad hasn't filled in the holes yet. The hole that opens into Sam's room is a big round opening.

"Sam," I whisper. "It's safe. He's passed out."

My brother's face, an ugly bruise on his left cheek, appears in the hole.

"Does it hurt?" I ask.

"No, not too bad. What about you?" Sam asks.

I touch the gash on my cheek. "It's okay."

"I'm freezing up here. The old prick took my blankets," Sam says. Sam hugs himself.

Mary tiptoes upstairs to the linen closet to get blankets.

"Do you want something to eat?"

"Yea, I'm starved."

"Okay. I'll get something."

Standing on a chair, I pass two thick blankets up through the hole to Sam. I pass a bowl of cereal, a peanut butter and honey sandwich, an apple, and a big glass of chocolate milk.

My sisters and I finish cleaning the kitchen. We do the dishes, put beer bottles back in their case, sweep the floor and wipe the cupboards.

Sam whispers, "I'm done, Becca." He passes the dirty dishes through the stovepipe hole to me. Mary takes them to wash. "Becca, I got to piss something wicked."

"Piss out the window."

"Can't. Shit-for-brains nailed the windows shut."

"Maybe I can get the lock open with a coat hanger or something."

"HELL NO! Don't even try. If you screw it up, we'll all get killed. Just find me something to piss in."

"Okay." I rummage in the cupboard and look for something nobody uses. My hand falls on the pot my mother uses to poach Dad's eggs on Sunday. She never uses that for anything else, and

Chapter 1: The Child

only Dad eats poached eggs. I pass the pot up through the hole to Sam.

"Becca, this is the old man's poached egg pot."

"I know. Piss in it. I promise not to hurt myself scrubbing it clean." We laugh wildly.

"Be quiet," Mary whispers loudly.

I sit on the chair. I listen to the piss hit the metal of the pot.

"All done. Here you go. Careful, don't spill it on yourself." I take the piss pot from my brother's hand. I walk to the outside door of the porch as though I carry something explosive. I reach the end of the porch and pitch the contents onto the snow. I give the pot a shake then run back inside shivering from the cold. "Where'd you throw it?" Sam asks.

"Off the porch."

"He might wonder in the morning where it came from."

"He won't remember, Sam. He'll think he did it hisself." We snicker. I put the pissy pot back in the cupboard without washing it. Mother will use it in the morning. I feel guilty. Then I think, this started over piss; it's only fair it ends pissy.

This afternoon Lisa accidentally wet herself. Dad said, "I'll cure your damn pissing problem once and for all." He pulled the belt from his pants and swung the buckle end at Lisa as she cowered near the kitchen table. I caught the first swing of the belt in my hand before it hit her. Dad yanked it loose before I could get my balance. The second swing hit me in the cheek and cut a long gash. I screamed. Lisa and Katie bawled loudly. Mary grabbed Dad's arm from behind and took an elbow to the eye.

The screaming and crying brought Sam in from outside. He lowered his head and charged. Dad fell against the wall. Sam rushed him again. Dad caught him that time. Sam took a couple of punches to the face. Sam let Dad drag him upstairs and lock him in his room.

The next day, we watch Dad slop poached egg onto toast at breakfast. Sam and I look at each other, then down at our cereal.

Dad says to Sam, "Bet you're hungry, son."

"Yea, Dad," Sam says flatly.

"Well, let that be a lesson to ya then. Don't defy your father and interfere when I am disciplinin' your sisters."

"Okay, Dad," Sam says.

"Let it be a lesson to you girls too."

"Okay, Dad."

"All I'm asking from you kids is a little respect."

Chapter 2: School

*Present a short, detailed account of
an experience you had or observed in school.*

The Eurocentric View

Jay Stephen

"Jay, let me touch your hair, please. Please?"

I hated them touching my hair.

"Okay, Craig, you can touch my hair." Craig was my best friend.

"That's wild. It feels like steel wool and bounces like a sponge. I bet you never have to comb that thing."

I said nothing.

We walked our way to our Catholic school in North York. My Catholic mother put me in the school. I tried to explain to her that all my neighbourhood friends went to public school. Why couldn't I? All I got for it was a stern look and "Don't get me mad, boy."

Three other Black people attended that school, but they were girls. I was the best athlete in my grade: the fastest runner, the best back flipper, and the toughest fighter. In short, I was cool. It was a survival thing: I had to be cool to take the ridicule. I got good grades, I got there on time, and I never skipped classes.

I hated my seventh-grade teacher, Ms. Dupuis. She had weird-looking blond hair, bulging blue eyes, and a rocky-looking face she got from plastic surgery to go with her frail, small-boned body. She smiled a strange half-smile all the time for no apparent reason.

Ms. Dupuis, like most teachers, wanted a class where the teacher talked, and the students listened. Otherwise, as she put it, "The student does not want to become part of the class." I questioned her about how things were done or how they came to be done that way. She said, "That's just how things are, Jay."

Chapter 2: School

One day an exchange between Ms. Dupuis and me went on until she said, "I don't know who you're trying to impress, Mr. Stephen, but you're taking up valuable class time. Now don't say another word, or you'll go to the office."

I pressed her, "You didn't answer my question yet, Ms. Du—"

"That's it. Down to the office. Let the principal explain to you how Columbus discovered the Caribbean."

"Spteews."

"Don't you dare kiss your teeth at me, young man!"

I walked downstairs to the office to meet Mr. Belouger, the vice-principal. Calm and down-to-earth, I never felt prejudice from him as I did from other teachers. Mr. Belouger got used to seeing me in his office. I even knew where he kept my files. He let me play with the mini-basketball net hanging over his trash can. I crunched up blank pieces of paper and took shots.

Knock, knock, knock. "Mr. Belouger, are you in there?"

"Yeah, Jay, come in. What's it about, today?"

"Sir, that lady is whacked. I asked during history class how Columbus could be the first to discover a place if he found people already there. She got all tight on me 'cause she couldn't explain."

Despite his smile, Mr. Belouger looked kind of stern. He leaned back in his big chair, rested his elbow on the arm of the chair, and looked at me with his hand on his chin. A minute passed. Finally, he said, "Come with me."

As we walked upstairs, I said, "It's like, she doesn't want to teach the truth, sir. What's the sense of learning a lie?"

Mr. Belouger and I walked into the classroom in the middle of a lesson. Everyone looked as we walked through the door. I felt the class's stare, but most of all, the stare of Ms. Dupuis.

"Can I see you for a moment, Laura?" Mr. Belouger said, "Wait here, Jay." As he spoke, I tried to determine his tone of voice, good or bad. I couldn't tell.

Mr. Belouger and Ms. Dupuis walked out into the hall. I waited for Caesar's thumb to point up or down. The class whispered. Everyone shushed one another, looking back at me.

Ms. Dupuis returned to the class.

Mr. Belouger stood in the doorway. With his forefinger, he called me out into the hall. Everything seemed like slow motion. I felt doomed. I took a last look at the class, then Ms. Dupuis. Her eyes looked evil.

In the hall, Mr. Belouger said, "Jay, we have to resolve this problem with you and Ms. Dupuis. I'm sorry I have to tell you this, but from now on, do not question Ms. Dupuis about such issues during class. When you confront her, you're discrediting the teacher in front of the rest of the class. Then it becomes a power struggle instead of a learning process. When you have a point to make or want to make something clearer for your understanding, please speak to the teacher after class, one-on-one."

"But what if she still gives me the same answer?"

"Then come to me, and we'll find the correct answer together. One more thing, Jay. Don't ever stop asking questions."

"I beg your pardon, sir?"

"Don't ever stop asking questions about things that don't make sense. You see, you were right about Columbus. He's a fraud. Unfortunately, history is regarded from a Eurocentric view, so people accept things despite their untruths. You'll learn about that in due time. Get back to class now, and remember what I said."

"Yes, sir." I walked back to my seat in class.

Chapter 2: School

Everyone seemed awed by my presence except Ms. Dupuis. She read from a history book, explaining, I think, how Jacques Cartier discovered Canada.

Piss

Sara Middleton

I wake up and feel the wetness beneath me. I scramble out of bed. The clock reads 5:56. I have half an hour until he wakes up. I can't believe I did it again.

I strip off my piss-soaked pyjamas and change into fresh clothes. I rip the sheets and blanket from the bed and use the dry parts to soak up the wet spots on the mattress. I toss the wet stuff on the floor and edge the window open to air out the room. The window squeaks. I listen for a sound from down the hall. I hear only my heart beating. I gather the soiled linens and cautiously open the door.

I pause at the top step, feel reassured when I hear snoring from down the hall, then tiptoe down the stairs. I toss the sheets into a pile in the far corner of the laundry room—I'll deal with them after school—and grab fresh ones. I go back to my bedroom, flip the mattress over and put clean sheets and a new blanket on the bed. I mess it up a little to look like it's been slept in. I grab Febreze from the kitchen and spray it lightly around the room.

I go to the bathroom and clean myself up. I get back to my room and hear the house begin to wake for the day. I hear Mom head to the bathroom. I peer around the door of my room and see Dad coming toward me on his way to the kitchen.

Terror runs through me. I stare at the floor. His feet stop inches away. I look up. His face contorts in disgust.

"You pissed yourself again, didn't you?"

My eyes meet the floor again.

Chapter 2: School

"This is why you have no friends. You don't deserve friends."

Dad walks to the kitchen. I turn around and slowly close my door. My cat, Red, sneaks inside before it shuts. I sit on the bed and cry. Red snuggles against me.

I wait until Dad leaves for work. I put my hair up in a ponytail and pull on jeans and a T-shirt. I eat a piece of toast. I don't tell Mom what happened. It's best not to.

I head out the door. Red follows me. I shoo him away. The other kids will think I'm weird. Red dodges from bush to bush and trails behind me most of the way to school. I lose sight of him as I cross the school parking lot.

The bell rings. I line up with the other fifth graders. Our teacher, Mrs. Eaton, leads us to our classroom.

What if they can smell pee on me? The other kids chatter with their friends. Mrs. Eaton tells them to quiet down. I sit at my desk near the back of the class. The desk next to mine, Kayla's desk, sits empty. I feel disappointment and relief.

Mrs. Eaton takes attendance. Kayla, late again, walks through the door with her shock of red hair. She takes her seat beside mine. I smile hesitantly. Kayla refuses to meet my eyes. Cold dread runs through me. Once class begins, Kayla rips a piece of paper from her notebook, writes something, and passes it to me.

"I'm mad at you," the note says.

I'm not sure what I did. But I have to make it better. My hand shakes as I write back, "I'm sorry."

Kayla writes another note. "If you don't make it up to me, I'm going to tell everyone your secret."

A few weeks ago, Kayla came to play at my house. She said she smelled something funny in my room. I told her the truth.

At recess, Kayla tells me I have to cancel my plans with Gemma tonight and tell Gemma, my only real friend, that I don't want to see her anymore. Kayla says this will make up for whatever I did to her. I beg Kayla to make it anything else.

"If you don't do it, Sara, I'm going to tell everyone you wet your bed like a baby. If you don't come and play with me after school, I'm going to hurt myself." I've seen Kayla repeatedly bang her head on the metal frame of her bed. "I do that when you make me angry."

The bell rings. It's time for gym class. I promise Kayla I'll find Gemma next recess and tell her she's not my friend anymore.

I dread gym. I feel exposed. I hate undressing in the change rooms. I never know what to wear, and I hate exposing my body to other girls. I lie to a couple of the girls and say I need to use the washroom. I change there. We get to the gym and sit in a circle. With my disjointed hips, I can't sit cross-legged like the other kids. I feel stupid. Teachers nag me to sit properly. I wish I could. I'm comfortable only with my legs to the side.

Before I sit down, the PA beeps for an announcement. We all listen. "Mr. Bole? Can you please send Sara down to the office?"

Everyone stares. My face flushes. I keep my head down and grab my bag and walk to the office. I peer through the glass door, afraid to knock. One of the secretaries, Mrs. Doyle, meets my eyes and motions me to enter. A small fourth grader sits in a chair and holds Red on her lap. Red looks ready to bite and tear at the kid. Red jumps out of the kid's arms and struts over to me. I pick him up. Mrs. Doyle looks at me, amused.

"This is the third time we've caught your cat walking down the halls of the school," she says. "He seems to be looking for you."

I stare at the floor and mumble, "I'm sorry."

Chapter 2: School

I ask if I can take Red home. Mrs. Doyle says yes. She knows I live just around the corner. "Come right back to school."

I clutch Red to my chest and walk out the doors. Red purrs. I kiss him on his head. Tears flow from my eyes.

I don't go back to school.

Operation Thumb Drive

Bilaal Mohamed

I sit on a plastic chair in the teacher's lounge. Notebooks, pencils, and calculators lie scattered across an oval oak desk with chips and scratches. Next to me, my friend and classmate, Dan, looks down and twiddles his thumbs.

Mrs. Thomas, our seventh-grade science teacher, sits across from Dan and me. She babbles and draws molecules on a fresh blank sheet. The fan on her old bulky Dell laptop roars.

Empty cubicles surround us. The scent of stale coffee beans fouls the air.

I turn my head and glance through the window. Flat, feathery clouds cross the sky and newly bloomed flowers rise from the grassy field and the tree leaves ruffle from the cool spring breeze and students flock out of the school and cars pack the roads. It's the end of the school day—except for Dan and me.

We spent the past few days getting after-school lessons from Mrs. Thomas to prepare for the next science test.

"What a beautiful day it is! Maybe if you guys paid attention in class instead of looking at your phones, maybe you would've passed your last test, and we all wouldn't be spending our afternoons here!" Mrs. Thomas says.

She draws hydrogen molecules on the blank paper and explains how hydrogen bonds form. I pretend to pay attention. I think about our big mission.

Mrs. Thomas hands us worksheets to practice on.

Chapter 2: School

"Alright, boys. I'm going to get a Lego molecule set from the science room. Make sure you finish the worksheets before I'm back."

She walks out of the lounge. Her high heels click-clack.

Dan and I wait. We hop out of our seats. I run around the table and sit on Mrs. Thomas' chair. Dan scurries to the side of the door and peaks his head out.

A week ago, Dan and I devised a scheme to pass the next science test. We would ask Mrs. Thomas for after-school lessons, slowly build her trust, and wait for the opportunity to steal the science test from her laptop. Dan's job is to look out for the teacher, and mine is to hack her computer. We called the mission Operation Thumb Drive.

I turn on her laptop, stick the USB in, and scour through the folders to find the test. I turn my head to Dan, who scans the hallways. His body twitches from nervousness.

I search through the laptop for the test paper. My palm sweat greases the mouse and keyboard. My right foot taps the marble floor. I feel nauseous.

"The coast is clear, man. Have you found the test yet?" Dan whisper-shouts at me.

"Not yet. Just be on the lookout."

My fingers poke faster at the keyboard to find the document. Multiple tabs open. I discover the Tests folder and scroll down to find the document titled "Science 7 term test 2." I open to verify that it's the paper.

"Dude, I found the test!"

"Great, dude. Just upload to the thumb drive."

I copy the file to the thumb drive. A progress bar pops up.

SLAM! The sound of a closing door echoes through the halls.

"Oh, shit, dude. It sounds like she's coming back. How long is it taking?"

"The progress bar is at ten percent right now."

Click-clack. The clacking gets louder with each step.

"Dude, she's gonna come at any moment. How long is left?"

"Fuck, dude. It's been stuck at thirty percent for a while."

Click-clack. My stomach sinks deeper. Tears run down my eyes and my lungs tighten and my heart races. The progress bar jumps to seventy percent.

Click-clack. I look at Dan. He ducks his head back to the classroom and presses against the wall.

"Dude, I fucking saw her walking to the classroom," his voice shakes.

Dan sprints to his desk. I turn back to the laptop screen. The progress bar hits a hundred percent. I yank the USB out of the computer and rush back to my seat.

Mrs. Thomas walks through the door with the Lego molecule box.

"Alright, are you guys done? Wait, why are worksheets blank?"

The lump in my throat blocks any words.

Mrs. Thomas squints at us. "Also, why are you guys breathing heavy?"

"Uhm, well, because we found the questions really hard, and uhm, we got really stressed out thinking about the test. Can you please help us since you are an amazing teacher?" Dan stutters.

"Oh well, of course!" Mrs. Thomas says.

She continues her lesson. We pulled off Operation Thumb Drive.

Chapter 2: School

On test day, I sit at my desk. Mrs. Thomas hands out the tests. Dan turns his head at me, his eyes full of horror.

Mrs. Thomas hands me the test. I scan through the paper. The questions are different. My stomach drops.

The Black Turban

A.R. Adam

Students from grades seven to twelve lined up in front of the main building in Pashma Qala Boys School in Chimtal, Afghanistan.

We stood in tens of perfect rows, shoulder-to-shoulder, like we were in the military. We held our breath and swallowed our words.

We didn't know why our school called for this assembly. All we knew was that our Principal, Mola Manan, would arrive soon with an important announcement.

Maybe a new order, a new rule, a new restriction, or maybe he will punish one of us. At our last assembly, two months earlier, we met Mola Manan for the first time. He spent the entire assembly threatening us with punishments if we broke any rules.

My younger brother, Eraj, stood beside me. He grabbed my hand and said, "Lala, I'm so scared!" Lala means "big brother" in Farsi.

"Don't worry brother, we will be okay. It's just going to be a new announcement," I said. I did not know if that was true.

The principal appeared on the stage. He marched to the podium. He stared at the students. His long hair and beard looked disheveled, as usual. Dark kolh eyeliner accentuated the whites of his eerie eyes. He wore a big turban, a long white outfit, and a black vest that stretched over his big tummy.

His holster carried a double magazine pistol. The gun poked under his vest. He cleared his throat, recited some verses, and gave

Chapter 2: School

a speech about the sacrifices he made while he fought up in the mountains against the government.

"The freedom you guys have today comes with a price, a huge price," he began. "This freedom comes as a result of my and my fellow Taliban members' sacrifices, and we all should be grateful for it." He picked up the bottle on the podium, sipped the water, put the bottle back, dried his lips with his hand, and continued.

"Okay, today I am announcing a new rule in our school. Every student has to wear a turban at school. This rule will be enforced from next week on."

The students remained in shocked silence.

The principal left the stage and we headed to our classes.

After school, Eraj and I rushed home and told Dad about the new rule. He shook his head. "It's a shame," he said.

The next day he bought us a pair of black turbans.

The following week, we prepared for school. The turban slouched over Eraj's tiny head. He looked like a miniature Taliban member. I decided to put my turban in my backpack and wear it when I arrived at school.

When we reached our school, I felt a voice within me forbid me from wearing the turban.

I listened to the voice.

In the middle of my class, the principal showed up. He never visited our classes before.

He walked to my desk. I was the only student in class with no turban. He stared into my eyes.

"Why didn't you wear the turban?"

"I'm so sorry, sir. I couldn't. But I have it in my backpack."

"Do you think you answered my question? Do you think that's a justification?"

Before I opened my mouth, he continued. "You are the captain of the class, Adam, you must be a role model to other students! Get up. Follow me."

My heart pounded. I stood up and followed him out of the classroom. I struggled to keep my balance.

We walked through the hall. He took long and fast strides. I raced to keep up with him. He turned left behind the library and stopped in front of his private room. He unlocked the door and pushed it open. The hinges squeaked. He stood in the doorway.

"Go in," he told me.

I entered the room, he followed me in, and closed the door.

I felt faint. The room blurred.

Will he kill me? Will he imprison me in his room?

"It's a shame, but we must follow what they ask," Dad's words echoed in my head.

"Okay, Mr. Adam. You choose how I should punish you for not wearing your turban."

My throat clogged. I could barely speak.

"I'm so sorry, sir. I will make sure to wear my turban at all times," I whispered.

"Look, I can beat you to death, and just ask your dad to come and take your body home if I want," he paused. "But I have decided to forgive you this time only under one circumstance."

His word choice increased my anxiety. I had heard the stories about his sexual affairs with teenagers when he was working as the head of Promotion of Virtue and Prevention of Vice office before he was appointed as our principal.

Chapter 2: School

"What circumstance, sir?" I finally asked.

"Don't worry, it's easy!" he continues. "Here is the deal. You know my son, Najibullah? He is your classmate. I will forgive you this time . . . ," he paused a few seconds. "I will forgive you this time, only if you help my son in the coming examinations."

My body relaxed, my heart steadied, and I nodded my head meekly.

The next day, and every day after, I wore that black turban to school.

~~~

Mola Manan remained as principal until the collapse of the Taliban in October 2011.

In 2021, the Taliban took over again. I fled to Canada.

My eldest sister is married and lives in America. My younger brother, a civil engineer, lives in Finland. My youngest brother graduated from college in Finland and lives in Helsinki.

My three other siblings still live with my parents in Kabul.

Sunday Afternoon

Paul Maka

The sound of the car pulling into the driveway takes my mind out of the world of Robertson Davies. A blue pen and a green highlighter rest on my knee. The car door slams shut. I close the book and listen. No voices. Dad must be home. My Sunday afternoon study period ends.

His boots thud up the front porch steps, then he kicks off the salt and slush. The screen door creaks open. Keys rattle. He always tries at least seven before finding the right one. The deadbolt slams back. The door swings open. The alarm box in the hall sounds its computerized warning beeps.

"Hello? Hello? Is anyone home?" Dad takes a few steps into the hall. "What are you doing in there?" He stands at the doorway.

I sit in the living room, the house's quietest and most comfortable place. "I have to finish this book for class tomorrow."

He grunts and walks away.

I pick *Fifth Business* back up. The main character was killed by the usual cabal: himself, first of all; by the woman he knew; by the woman he did not know; by the man who granted his innermost wish; and by the inevitable fifth, the denouement.

Who were the two women? I flip back a few pages and reread a selection.

"Oh, Paul, don't rest your feet on there! What are you doing?"

Dad stands in the doorway again. My feet rest on the solid oak coffee table. I feel comfortable.

Chapter 2: School

"Can you leave me alone? I'm trying to get some work done!"

He walks away and mutters, "Work? That's work?" His sarcastic laughter trails from the room.

I grab my books, pen and highlighter and storm down the basement stairs. The only English class Dad took was designed for engineers. He laughs when he tells the story. "We never even read the book. We all just copied off the smart guys. Ha. They just sat in the cafeteria with their notebooks spread open on the table, and we sat around writing everything down. You didn't have to do any work, and you still passed."

I am in the English Specialist program at UTM. I have to read at least four books a week to keep up.

I turn on my computer. The fan whirs and the tower vibrates. I wedge a book up against it to stop the noise. Upstairs, Mom arrives home. Dad yells at her. He complains about my little brother Michael. "All he ever does is watch TV."

I know this song. I can't hear Mom's tired response. It doesn't matter. It's the same fight every day. Michael maintains a B average in school.

I flip open my notebook and find my assignment: Write a detailed account of family life. I type a few points.

> "   and what about Paul? I never see him doing any work. All he does all day is play computer games. What kind of courses does he take? I wish I had classes like that when I was in university."

Dad comes down to check up on me as I type my essay. The screensaver comes on when I stop to think. He thinks screensavers are computer games. My heart pounds. My hands tremble. I want to yell something at him.

Instead, I write.

The Pantsing

Madeleine Brown

"Pantsing? What's that?"

We grade-eight girls stand in a tight pack next to our school, Adam Scott Collegiate Vocational Institute.

"I mean it. What is pantsing?" I say again.

"It's when you pull someone's pants down, just suddenly, in front of everyone!" Lauren laughs. "Like this—"

She lunges for the waistband of my pants. I dash away.

"Lauren!" I giggle.

"Yeah, Lauren," Kirstyn cries and teasingly reaches out for Lauren's jeans. She pulls her hands back at the last second.

We break from our clump and run around the schoolyard threatening to pants one another. We end up giggling in a pile on the ground.

"I would pants someone," Lauren says as the laughter subsides. "I mean it."

"I dare you, then!" I blurt. "When recess is over and everyone's at their lockers getting stuff for their next class, you pull down some kid's pants."

Silence. Everyone's eyes fall on Lauren. She agrees to the challenge.

The lunch bell rings, and we walk into the school. The weight of the dare slows our pace.

"Dylan. He's wearing basketball shorts, so it'll be easy," Lauren states matter-of-factly.

Chapter 2: School

We stand alongside the main hallway wall eyeing our classmates as they open their lockers and retrieve binders and books. Dylan and I, best friends from senior kindergarten until the end of grade five, spent birthday parties, playdates and recess together. I swallow nervously. My throat tightens. We wait for someone to speak.

"Lauren, you don't have to do it," I say. "I was joking. Don't."

"Yeah, no one cares!"

"Forget it. It's stupid."

Lauren sprints across the hallway, arms outstretched and pulls Dylan's green shorts to the floor. His baby blue boxers shine in the dimness of the hallway.

Dylan's face reddens. He drops his books and yanks his shorts back up. The excitement of the pantsing comes and goes in a single second. Nobody, amid the bustle of the hallway, even notices. My eyes dart toward the class clown, Kevin Blunck. Nothing. Cameron Oles and Brad MacLeod, two boys in my homeroom class, walk by oblivious. We feel disappointment and relief.

Teachers, however, pop out into the hallway from their classrooms as if they can sense misbehaviour. Disapproval marks their tired faces.

Ms. Scott marches all of us to the principal's office. She drags Lauren, still standing in awe, with us.

No one speaks.

Going to the principal's office usually means reading the daily announcements over the PA system or receiving words of congratulations on good work. I've never had to visit about bad behaviour. My hands feel clammy, and my face flushed and hot.

The vice principal, Ms. Russell, calls us into her office. She lectures us. How do we think Dylan feels now? What if we'd been in his shoes? How embarrassing! Her scolding rattles on. We hang our heads and hold back tears.

It gets worse.

Ms. Russell orders us to call our parents and inform them of what happened. "Right now."

I feel stupid explaining pantsing to Mom as my friends and the vice principal listen. "It's when you pull someone's pants down, just all of a sudden, in front of everyone," I mumble into the receiver.

Ms. Russell instructs us to report to the office for detention the following day at lunch. We leave in pained silence.

The janitor greets us coldly when we arrive for our detention. He hands us each a broom and tells us to sweep the parking lot for the entire lunch hour. "Every grain of sand, every piece of garbage."

I stare at the glowing sun as I sweep through my first and last detention.

Miss Fitzgerald

Ebi Agbeyegbe

It's almost noon on yet another bright, sunny day at St. Jacobs High School in Lagos, Nigeria. I sit at the back of the room, just the way I like. A clock ticks away at the front of the class, pictures hang on the walls, writing fills the chalkboard. Students chat quietly.

My friends and I look forward to noon when all grade-five students get an hour for lunch. Some of us play in the spacious field before we return to our classes.

Although I sit at the back, I have a great view of Miss Fitzgerald, my favourite teacher. I admire the way she teaches with such passion. Other students glance at the clock, but I enjoy English class the most. I feel comfortable, and I like the lessons.

When the bell rings, everyone packs up their stuff and rushes into the hall towards the cafeteria.

"Don't forget to do the readings on Chapter Five for the next class," Miss Fitzgerald yells.

I wait a few seconds and stand at the back of the class. The standard school uniform makes me look presentable—a long-sleeved white shirt, green shorts, and black shoes. I roll up the sleeves of my shirt and approach Miss Fitzgerald. My body feels hot. My palms sweat. Only she and I remain in the classroom.

Miss Fitzgerald's head, her long curly hair pulled back in a neat bun, looks down at the table where she grades some papers.

I reach the table, inhale deeply, and then exhale. "Hi, Miss."

She jerks up slightly. "Hello, John. How may I help you?"

I look around and see the textbook on her desk. "I wanted to ask about the assignment."

She looks at me and smiles. Everything seems to slow down. The hairs on my skin stand up.

"What exactly would you like me to explain about the homework?" She reaches over, opens the textbook, and flips the pages to the assigned chapter.

"I wanted to know what Shakespeare meant in the story when he said, 'O Romeo, Romeo! Wherefore art thou Romeo?'"

Miss Fitzgerald comes closer to show me the quote. When she stands up, I notice her light brown dress. It looks perfect on her. She explains the passage, but I can only think about how nice she smells.

She finishes and says, "Do you understand now?"

"Yes. You smell nice, Miss."

She smiles wide and says, "Thank you."

I shuffle back to my desk to get my backpack. I tell myself I have to say something else, or I'll look lame. On my way out, I walk past her desk and say, "I like your dress, Miss."

She grins, gets up from her seat, walks over to me, and kisses me on the cheek.

I take a deep breath, smile and say, "Thank you, Miss." I run out of the class towards the field to my friends.

For the rest of the day, I think about Miss Fitzgerald. I get to my dorm, and I decide to write her a poem. I stay awake until two in the morning, perfecting each word.

The next day when English class ends, I wait behind. The last student leaves. I bring out the poem. Mr. Malcolm, my math teacher, strolls into the room.

Chapter 2: School

He walks to Miss Fitzgerald's desk and kisses her on the cheek. "Ready for lunch, babe?"

The poem drops from my hand.

Miss Fitzgerald sees me. She heads toward me and appears to utter some words. I pack up my poem, books, pens and glasses. She calls out my name. I storm out of the classroom.

Choke

Christina Hunter

"What if someone sees us?" I ask.

While all the other grade-eight students sit cross-legged in a stuffy auditorium, my friends and I huddle behind the portables of St. Aaron Elementary School. We rub our hands together for warmth, wipe our noses on our sleeves, blow clouds as we speak, and sniffle between words.

"Everyone's at the assembly. No one's gonna see us. Besides, Johnny's watching for teachers," Graham says.

"I'm just not sure this is a good idea," Adam mutters, hands in his pockets.

"Don't be a pussy," Chris says.

Graham spits into the snow. "You said you'd do it. She'll be here any minute, so make up your fucking mind."

"What if something goes wrong?" Adam says.

"It won't."

"How do you know?"

"Because she's done this, like, a million times."

"And nothing's ever gone wrong?"

"Never."

"She's coming," Johnny calls over.

"Does someone else wanna go first? I wanna see what happens," Adam says. He sweats despite the cold.

"What a loser," Chris laughs.

"Guys, don't force him," I say. "If he doesn't wanna do it—"

Chapter 2: School

"Aw, standing up for your boyfriend?"

"He's not my boyfriend."

"How cute."

"He's not my boyfriend. Anyways, Adam, it's no big deal. We've all done it."

"She's here!" Johnny says.

Hoami saunters over, seething with sex and confidence. Beautiful, charming, outspoken and stupid, she is every eighth-grade boy's wet dream.

"What's up?"

"Adam's scared." Graham laughs. He crosses his arms so that his biceps bulge.

"I am not. Let's do it."

Hoami signals to Graham and Chris. They move to support Adam. Hoami sashays forward until she is within inches of Adam's face. She runs her tongue across her lips. Adam swallows. She places her hands on his neck, leans in, tilts his head back, and presses on the veins in his neck. He blinks violently. The whites of his eyes dart wildly.

One minute passes. Adam reddens.

"Pressing," Hoami soothes. "Hold your breath, don't fight it. Don't fight, don't fight, don't . . . there you go."

Two minutes pass. Adam's legs tremble. Three minutes. Adam's eyes roll back.

"Ease him down, guys," Hoami says. "Be careful. Watch his head."

"Pasty little shit, eh?" Chris jokes.

"A lightweight, too," Graham adds. "That was . . . what? Two minutes?"

"Three," I say.

"About as long as he'd last in bed," Chris snickers.

"Shut up," I say. "He's waking up."

"How ya feeling?" Hoami asks.

"I'm fucking tripping right now." Adam's eyes, glazed and unfocused, roll from the sky to the ground and back to the sky. "Do it again."

"You can't," I say. "Adam, you've got to wait before you can do it again. You have to let the oxygen back into your brain."

"It's fine. I'm fine. I feel great. Do it again."

"You heard him," Graham says.

"Seriously guys, I don't think—"

"Hold him up, then. I can't do it myself."

"Guys, c'mon."

"You got him?" Graham and Chris support Adam's body between them. He lies back into their arms.

"I think you should wait," I say.

"I think you should stop spazzing," Chris spits.

Hoami moves in again. "Three . . . two . . . one," she counts. In less than two minutes, Adam's out. He sways, slumps, and falls. His body crumples onto the asphalt.

"Shit!"

"What the fuck are you doing?" I shout.

"Sorry! My arm slipped!" Chris says.

"He could crack his fucking skull!"

"He's fine. Relax," says Hoami.

"Both of you, shut up," Graham says.

I look at Adam. My stomach churns. "Why is he twitching like that?" No one answers. "Why is he twitching like that?"

Chapter 2: School

Johnny rushes over from his guard post, cell phone poised and filming.

"I don't think he's okay. Something's wrong. Is he seizing?"

"No," Hoami huffs. "Just wait. It'll stop."

We watch. I hold my breath. I pray.

"See?" Graham shoves me. "He stopped. Problem solved."

"'Kay. But he's supposed to wake up now, right?"

"Just give it a sec."

"How long is it supposed to take?"

"Would you shut the fuck up?"

"Relax," Hoami says.

"Something's wrong."

"Nothing's wrong."

"He's not waking up. Johnny. Get a teacher."

"Are you fucking stupid?" he yells. "We'll get suspended."

"What if he dies? We'll go to jail!"

"Shut up," Chris says. "You're spazzing about nothing. He'll be fine."

"He's fucking purple!"

"Would you shut the fuck up so I can fucking think?"

I've never seen Hoami lose her cool. It feels gratifying. I look down at Adam. He looks like he's already dead. I taste bile in the back of my throat.

"I'm gonna go get a teacher."

"Don't you dare!" Chris says. He turns to Hoami. "What do we do?"

"Fuck if I know. They always just . . . wake up."

"We should get a teacher," Graham relents.

"Fuck." Hoami's eyes water. "Shit, fuck, fuck. Does anyone know CPR?"

Silence.

"We can't let anyone find out," Johnny says.

Graham takes out his cell phone and dials 911. "We're so fucked."

I run to get a teacher.

~~~

The principal suspended us for a week. When Graham, Chris, Johnny and I returned to school, we didn't talk about what happened. We didn't talk to each other at all.

The school board expelled Hoami.

Adam survived.

I learned later that the high Adam experienced resulted from millions of brain cells dying. I learned later that Adam suffered massive brain trauma. He never came back to that school. I never saw Adam again.

Lakeview Indian Day School

Marylou Ceccile Debassige

Manitoulin Island circa 1965

Real fast, I turn around in my desk to look at my cousin. He says something in our Odawa and Ojibwe language.

This is a mistake.

The teacher, Miss McNulty, walks with a limp. She uses a cane. We all jump when she hits a desk with it. I'm sure the cane would cry if it had feelings. She doesn't need her cane this time. She stands in front of me and waves a new yardstick.

Another yardstick. How many did she break so far—on someone or on the blackboard?

Crack! Across my knuckles. It happens fast. I half cry out. I try to hold it in. A big lump rises from inside, pauses at my throat, and stops briefly at my nose. My eyes hurt. Tears roll down my face. My nose drips.

"Mary Louise, you must never speak that whatever language again! Never! Never! It is not a proper language! You must forget it totally! Speak English only! Hear me?"

She shakes me by the shoulders.

"Yes, ma'am."

She glares at me.

"Repeat after me. I will not speak Indian ever again."

I chokingly speak every word after her because I am scared she will hit me with her yardstick or her pointer stick.

But my habit is to speak Anishinaabemowin and English together. I don't understand why speaking Anishinaabemowin is wrong. Miss McNulty makes my mother language sound evil and ugly.

Catechism begins another day at this Indian day school.

Miss McNulty asks, "Who made you, Jane?"

Jane looks around and says, "God made me."

"Dick, where is God?"

Dick answers fast. "God is everywhere." I look at Dick in wonder. He is smart.

"Mary Louise, say 'The Hail Mary' in front of the class."

I get up in front of the classroom and try to keep my eyes straight ahead. I'm ready to die. Miss McNulty will kill me if I forget a word or a line of this English prayer. She tells me to fold my hands.

I start.

> *Hail Mary, full of Grace*
> *The Lord is with Thee.*
> *Blessed art thou amongst women,*
> *Blessed is the fruit of . . .*

I wish I could say this prayer in Anishinaabemowin. N'mishomiss, my grandfather and the Chief of the West Bay Reservation for many years, taught me to pray in Anishinaabemowin. N'mishomiss is a devoted Roman Catholic.

This morning, I feel scared as I try to remember. I've said this prayer at The Legion of Mary, the religious group on the reservation. There, we pray together. They don't force me to say every word or sentence. I feel safe and happy there. This morning, my mind

Chapter 2: School

empties, and I forget. Nobody is allowed to help me. I have to say this prayer by myself. For sure, this is doomsday.

"Mary Louise, stay after school and write The Hail Mary on all the blackboards and then stand in the cloakroom and repeat it until I return."

I write until my arm feels like falling off. At last, the blackboards are full of Hail Marys. I say it aloud over and over again in the cloakroom. I am alone. I feel weird and sick. Miss McNulty does not come back. Maybe she forgets I am still here. I need her permission to go home. I have chores to do. I have to bring in firewood and feed the pigs.

I knock on Miss McNulty's kitchen door. I picture her eyeballs rolling. I am not used to her loud, screechy voice. She sounds like the pigs we kill on our farm.

The door finally opens, and out comes Miss McNulty, almost pushing me down. Straight for the classroom goes bent-over Miss McNulty, like "the crooked man who walked a crooked mile." Her legs or whatever must be bothering her again. She checks the blackboard carefully. She orders me to sweep the steps.

"Make sure you sweep the corners properly. Then you may go."

I run all the way home without stopping. I will tell someone what happened at school today. I know my mother does not like to hear something like this. One of her rules is "Children should be seen and not heard." She nearly always listens to other people's sayings.

My mother attended St. Joseph's Catholic Residential School in Spanish, Ontario. They kept her in that school from when she was a little girl until she was almost twenty.

My mother did not talk to me about her school. She treated it like a secret. Sometimes, when she didn't know I listened, I heard her speak with her friends about that school. The nuns grabbed her hair and beat her all over her body with sticks. They forced her to work every day. She baked bread, did the laundry, washed the floors, and weeded the garden.

Like Miss McNulty, my mother hits me, except she uses long branches from trees. I try to stay away from her, not tell her anything, even when I know it's the truth.

N'mishomiss is different. His rule is: tell the truth always.

"Mishomiss! Mishomiss! Where are you?"

I run to the barn and find him in his workshop. He fixes Queen's harness. Queen is one of his ponies.

Mishomiss looks at me with a question in his eyes. He sits down, takes his pipe out, and fills it with tobacco. He points to the glass bottle filled with sweet tea. I fill two cups with tea. He reaches out his hand to take one cup. I keep the other and sit in front of him in one of the chairs he made out of tree stumps.

N'mishomiss looks at me and stays quiet while I tell him about my day at school. When I finish talking, he puffs his pipe. He is deep in thought. I wait for him to finish thinking. He takes his pipe out of his mouth.

"Are you telling me the truth, Brother (his nickname for me)?"

"Aehn (yes), Mishomiss." This time he does not laugh or smile as he does when he catches me telling him big or funny stories.

~~~

Soon, a younger, kinder teacher takes Miss McNulty's place at Lakeview Indian Day School.

Chapter 3: Family

Present a picture of life in a family. Detail an event or chain of events you have experienced or observed.

The Good Boy

M.A. Najfi

Mr. and Mrs. Rodriguez were the oldest couple on Nairn Circle in Milton, Ontario. Whenever a moving van appeared, they were the first people to walk over to greet the new neighbours. Mrs. Rodriguez always held a tin tray in her palms, while Mr. Rodriguez, with one arm around her waist, rang the doorbell.

They brought tuna casserole, gazpacho, tamales, or whatever else Mrs. Rodriguez had cooked up. Mrs. Rodriguez loved to cook and loved to share the fruit of that love with everyone.

One winter morning, after a harsh snowstorm, I stepped out to shovel our driveway. Across the street, Mr. and Mrs. Rodriguez struggled to clear the deep snow off their sidewalk. Their arms trembled with each shovelful. Mr. Rodriguez groaned in the winter chill.

It pained me to watch them. I walked across the street with my shovel. "Please, go on inside," I said. "It's way too cold. I'll finish this off."

Mrs. Rodriguez murmured Spanish words to her husband in a sweet tone. Mr. Rodriguez patted me hard on the back. His face wrinkled with a smile visible even behind the COVID face mask. "Such a good boy!"

The two of them went inside. I finished cleaning off the sidewalk and their driveway and then turned to head back home.

Mrs. Rodriguez scuttled out of their door and yelled and flailed her arms. "Mi hijo, wait!" she called out. She slowly climbed down the stairs to meet me.

Chapter 3: Family

She carried a small foil container. She held it toward me and lifted the lid to reveal hot churros, Milka bars, and other Spanish treats. "Please take something back for you. Thank you. Such a good boy!"

My cheeks flushed. "Mrs. Rodriguez, I can't."

"Be a good boy, now." She clicked her tongue. "This is my thank you."

I took the container from her hands and headed home.

That was my first encounter with them. I continued to shovel their driveway every snowfall and, admittedly, enjoyed delicious treats. What started with snow and food turned into admiration and respect for the Rodriguezes.

After that harsh winter, the only time I saw them was when I rode my bike to school. Every morning, I passed by the two of them sitting outside on their patio swing—Mr. Rodriguez reading the newspaper with his legs over Mrs. Rodriguez's lap, she caressing and massaging his knees while she sipped her morning tea.

"Good morning, Mr. and Mrs. Rodriguez!" I would call from my bike.

Mr. Rodriguez always smiled and waved, and Mrs. Rodrigues always yelled out, "Good morning, you good boy!"

I would chuckle and ride on. I don't think they remembered my name. So I became The Good Boy.

When the weather grew colder, I stopped seeing them outside on their patio swing. After the first snowfall of the winter, I crossed the street to clean their driveway and sidewalk. No footprints appeared in the snow, but I did not think much about it. After I finished, I walked back to my house. I listened for Mrs. Rodroguez to call after me. I heard nothing.

A clean blanket of knee-deep snow covered their driveway when the snow fell next. I shovelled the Rodriguez's as usual when I heard a door slam shut behind me.

"What are you doing?"

I turned to face Mr. Rodriguez. He looked at me with his face contorted and his eyes bloodshot.

"I was just . . . " I mumbled, confused and thrown off guard by the agency in his tone. "Sorry, I'll head back home."

Mr. Rodriguez looked me up and down. His features slackened before he grimaced and motioned me towards him. "No, please come here. Just wait a minute."

I walked up to the porch. He closed the door and headed back inside. A few seconds later, he returned holding one of Mrs. Rodriguez's classic foil containers in his hand.

"Maria would want you to have this," he stammered. He looked up at the sky and avoided my gaze.

I felt a heavy silence.

"You don't need to shovel our driveway anymore, okay. I'm moving in a week, back to Vaughan to live with our son."

I blinked at him. I waited for him to say what I couldn't fathom.

"Maria . . . my wife . . . passed away three weeks ago." His red eyes filled with water.

Tears tugged at the corners of my eyes. I held them back. I smiled awkwardly as Mr. Rodriguez handed me a foil container.

I lurched forward and hugged Mr. Rodriguez tightly.

Chapter 3: Family

He groaned, stiffened, then wrapped his arms around me.
"You're a good boy, you know." He patted my back.
I buried my face in his warm jacket.

Little Bird

Phoebe Chin

I don't know why Mom is yelling. I've stopped keeping track. Probably something I forgot to do. Dammit. Now I remember. I forgot to throw out the uneaten half of my sandwich at lunchtime. My eyes fall to my lunch bag on the kitchen counter, zipper open like a gaping red mouth. The cellophane-wrapped half-sandwich lies inside. The sandwich seems to say: *You knew this would happen. You should've just eaten me.*

I realize Mom is still yelling at me when she slaps my cheek with the back of her hand and I feel the air from the swing swish past my ears. Mom grips my arm and drags me down the hallway, her thick plastic slippers thwacking the hardwood floor. She rounds the corner of the bathroom and pulls me with her. The metal door latch catches my hip, tears my thin cotton shirt, and grazes the skin underneath.

Mom hurls me to the floor. "You are a spoiled and ungrateful child. Think about what you have done."

Mom slams the door shut, rattling the mirror in the cabinet beside me. The lights remain off. The crack under the door lets in some light, so I can still see a little. The heating vent hums. I feel the chenille bath rug under my legs and nail clippings that missed the garbage can. I use the pads of my fingers to press onto the clippings and lift them to the bin. They prick my fingers.

The bathroom smells like burnt hair and Mom's cherry-blossom-scented shampoo. I curl my legs beneath me and hug myself.

Chapter 3: Family

I will myself to stay still. I pretend my thighs are a piano keyboard and tap my fingers through the air, practising the sonatina I learned last week. I don't know what time it is. I don't know how long she wants me in here.

I hear dishes break, and porcelain clatter on the ceramic floor in the kitchen. Water runs. She may be washing dishes, but it sounds like she's throwing plates from the sink onto the floor.

A squawk comes from the living room. One of Mom's co-workers gave us the gift of a canary last week. I named the canary Aden. Not used to the noise yet, Aden emits indignant chirps of displeasure.

I hear Mom stomp across the living room. The cage crashes to the floor. Birdseed scatters over the hardwood. Aden cries out. I hear his wings beat against the bars.

You'll have to get used to it, little bird—just like the rest of us.

Grandfather

Simin Emadzadeh

I hold Grandpa's hand, and Mom holds his other hand as we walk him to his room. His knee trembles with every step he takes. I feel the wrinkles on his hand. Loose skin hangs from his arms. He looks fragile. We hold him tight so that he doesn't fall.

My grandparents' apartment in Iran has three bedrooms and a living room with a long, narrow hallway that leads to the dining room. The kitchen opens to a TV room where the dinner table sits.

It takes us almost fifteen minutes to walk from the bathroom to Grandpa's bed. His eyes look tired, and his hands feel cold. Mom dries droplets of sweat from his forehead with a towel and then kisses him. He looks at Mom's face with his big bug eyes.

"Where is Banoo?" he asks.

"Dad, she went to get your prescription," Mom says. "She will be home soon."

"Banoo," he calls out for Grandma. His eyes scan the room.

"I just told you, Baba, she will be back very soon."

Grandpa looks up at Mom again, then looks away.

I take the towel back to the bathroom while Mom sets up Grandpa's diaper. She never lets me stay in the room when she changes his diaper. I see Mom bent forward, holding her back with both hands. Pain lines her face. Mom always has backaches but won't let me help her change Grandpa's diapers. I help Mom put his clothes on.

Chapter 3: Family

We lay Grandpa down on his bed. Mom massages his feet. The doctor said massage helps his blood circulation since he can't walk much anymore. I put moisturizer on his dry feet and rub them.

"Banoo... Banoo... Banoo," Grandpa shouts again and tries to hold his head up.

"Baba Bozorg, she's not home yet," I tell him.

"Where did she go?" he asks. "Why did she leave me?"

"She didn't leave you. She went to buy your medications. She will come back soon."

I rub his hand.

"I have to finish cooking, Simin," Mom says and heads to the kitchen.

Grandpa looks agitated. His trembling arms can barely pull up his blanket. It hurts to watch.

At one time, Grandpa was the most intimidating person I had ever known. A strict dictator, he never let anyone get away with a single breach of his rules. Everyone respected and feared him.

We had fun at his house only when he wasn't home. He wouldn't let us play and be loud. During meals, we had to sit at the dinner table. No one was allowed to leave without his permission—even when the phone rang. "Whoever it is, cut it soon and come back to the table," he yelled at Grandma.

Grandpa set a strict curfew for Mom, my brothers, my cousins and me. No one was allowed to come home later than eight at night. We all hated his strictness. It was torture to shut the lights at ten and stay quiet. His presence triggered tension and fear.

"Banoo," he shouts again.

"Baba Bozorg, she is on her way home."

Grandpa looks into my eyes. "Who are you?" he asks.

Grandfather

"I am your grandchild, Simin," I say softly.

He looks away. He pushes his sheet off the bed to the floor and tries to sit up. I pick up the sheet and sit him upright.

"Are you hungry, Baba Bozorg?" I ask. He traces the flower patterns on the sheet with his fingers and pushes them away again.

"Banoo," he calls. "Where is Banoo?"

The Door

Rahul Sethi

A gale wind blew off the door of our basement apartment. As Mom carried in groceries, a gust of wind wrenched the door and hinges from the frame.

The Punjabi landlord didn't speak about the many flaws in the basement apartment's design when my parents, aunt, and uncle looked over the place before we signed the six-month rental agreement and moved in. Now, he stands outside with Mom and considers the exposed entranceway to our apartment and the door on the ground. His tongue slips loose. "Everything they did backward. You can't trust Punjabis to do a proper job." He shakes his head. "I should have got Italians."

The landlord counts out the positive traits of white folks by touching the tip of his thumb to the creases of his pinkie. "They're always professional. They do the job right the first time and never complain about the work or how much they're getting paid. Our folk are a sneaky lot."

Mom nudges the door with her foot.

"And you know . . . " A cold wind sweeps over the landlord. He wraps his scarf tighter around his neck and shoves his hands under his arms. "The idiots. When they laid the cement for this," he stomps his foot on the cement walkway that leads to the basement, "they made it slope toward the house. It hasn't happened this winter yet—and I hope it never happens—but it always happens that snow leaks through the walls onto the floor, wetting my carpet."

The Door

It is ten in the evening when Mom finally comes in from her talk with the landlord. He told her it was impossible to attach the door without replacing the doorframe. The wood that the hinges screw into had snapped into splinters and woodchips. The landlord said Mom would have to buy the new frame since she had let go of the door. "You should have held onto it tightly so that it wouldn't blow off in that wind," he said. "You should have been more careful."

It's too late to go to the hardware store. Aikenhead's at Warden and Eglinton closed at nine. Mom has to wait until tomorrow. Besides, Papa and Gulu Uncle drove the Honda Civic to work and won't be home until seven in the morning.

Every evening, Papa and Gulu Uncle head to the printing factory carrying their tiffin boxes, steel lunchboxes with four containers that latch together—one for rice, one for curry, one for roti, and one for a sweet dish. They work the night shift in a factory at Midland and Ellesmere, printing synthetic Nike, Reebok and Adidas logos on T-shirts, shorts and hats. Papa sometimes brings home Nike T-shirts and shorts for my brother Rohit and me. He brings home shirts that can't be sent to the stores because they have a rip or tear. The logos usually fade after a second wash.

Mom grabs a roll of Scotch tape from a drawer in the kitchen. She tells us to put on our coats, hats, gloves, extra pants, and socks until she and Babita Aunty fix the door. We make breath clouds while we slide into additional layers.

Babita Aunty wraps another blanket around baby Nitin and squeezes chubby little Nikita into woollen socks, a jacket and snow pants. She changes into winter clothes and climbs the stairs to the entrance door. As she walks up, Babita Aunty rolls her long hair into

Chapter 3: Family

a bun, pulls out a pen from her pocket and pokes it through her hair to hold the bun in place.

Wind gusts into the basement as Mom and Babita Aunty struggle to fit the door back into the frame. Mom lifts the door from the ground and manoeuvres it to where it once stood. From inside the basement, she grips the doorknob and pulls the heavy metal door into place.

"Babita." Mom gestures to the doorknob. "Hold this."

Babita Aunty steadies the door as Mom runs Scotch tape wall to wall and makes a web of tape to hold the door in the frame. Mom tells Babita Aunty to let go of the doorknob. Moments later, the heavy door peels itself away from the web of tape and falls to the cement walkway outside with a thud. We cringe. Mom crosses her arms over her waist and then raises a fist to her lips.

Mom and Babita Aunty rummage through the basement and return with a stack of boxes—cereal boxes, Chiquita Banana cardboard boxes from grocery shopping at No Frills, empty Bata shoe boxes—and plastic bags. Mom gives Rohit, little Nikita and me each a bowl of Count Chocula for dinner and adds the box to the pile.

Mom and Babita Aunty tape the collection into a collage the size of our entrance door. They carry it up the stairs and cover the open entranceway. Mom runs the Scotch tape from wall to wall, making another web of tape.

The tape holds. But after a few gales, the makeshift door bows inward the tape pops free. A powerful gust blows one side of the door off the wall. It flaps like a flag in the wind.

Mom grabs nails and thumbtacks from a drawer in the kitchen, picks up the hammer from where it lies on the shoe rack and runs to the entrance. She nails and thumbtacks the door to the doorframe.

She stands at the door for a few minutes, the hammer dangling from her thin hand.

The door rustles—but it holds.

We all sit on the couch in our small living room—Mom, Babita Aunty, Rohit and little Nikita. A portable heater in the living room rotates and radiates heat. Baby Nitin lies asleep in his crib, wrapped in three blankets with a little toque on his head.

Mom puts on a video of *TaleSpin* episodes that Rohit recorded on the VCR. She takes off our jackets and extra layers and covers us with a blanket. We huddle on the couch and watch Baloo and Kit outwit Don Karnage. We all doze while dogs, tigers and hyenas fly propeller planes and seek to steal pricey cargo from a pilot bear and his sidekick cub. We sleep through the night on the couch.

Mom and Babita Aunty awake in the morning to see Papa and Gulu Uncle standing in the living room, holding their tiffin boxes.

"What happened?" Papa gestures to the entrance with a nod. "What happened to the door? We had to tear that thing open to get inside."

Papa and Gulu Uncle have torn a wide gap in the centre of the door, large enough for them to step through.

"Did you show the landlord?"

Mom gets out from under the blanket. Rohit, little Nikita and I look up. "Come," Mom says. She puts on her winter jacket and boots. She stretches out her hand and asks for the keys to the Honda Civic. "We have to go."

Two weeks after the door blew off, the snow melts. The basement carpet soaks up a minor flood and drenches our socks when we walk.

The Visit

Mark Bialy

I sit on the couch in the family room and sip hot tea. My eyes watch *SportsCentre* on the TV, but my mind wanders to what Grandpa will look like when he visits today. I'm fifteen years old. I've never seen my dad's father, not even in pictures.

Grandpa lives in Toronto, where Dad grew up. I don't know much about Dad's side of the family. He has two brothers. His mother died before I was born, and his father has lived alone ever since. If it wasn't for Mom nagging Dad to invite Grandpa over, I don't think I would be meeting him.

Dad, smelling of Ralph Lauren Polo cologne, grabs his wallet off the counter and the keys to the Mercedes-Benz. "I'll be back in a few hours." He rarely drives the Mercedes.

Two hours later, Dad calls on his cell and says they're almost home. My sister Amanda and I hustle upstairs to our rooms and change into church clothes, for me, khaki pants, a white dress shirt, and a blue argyle sweater.

Mom cooks meatloaf, mashed potatoes, and cauliflower in the kitchen. "Amanda! Marek!" Mom shouts. "Can one of you set the table?"

I take five gold-rimmed plates from the oak cabinet and place them on the dining room table. I arrange silver cutlery around each plate—fork on the left, knife on the right, dessert spoon above. Amanda sets the napkins and glasses. I open the blinds.

The doorbell rings. Amanda and I eye each other.

Mom opens the front door. "Why, hello there!" Mom says. "It's so good to meet you finally! I'm Peter's wife, Margaret."

Mom and Grandpa exchange kisses.

"Yes, yes, Margaret. I am so glad to be here and see you," Grandpa says, "You are so beautiful."

I look at Amanda, and we inch out of the dining room. A slender man, six inches shorter than Dad, stands inside the door. He wears a baseball cap, leather jacket and loafers. Grandpa's small head, narrow eyes and sharp nose contrast with Dad's big head, wide-set eyes and round nose.

"Dziadek! Hi," I say.

I hug Grandpa. Amanda does the same. He squints and cranes his neck toward us. "My goodness, you kids are so tall! Marek, you look just like your father!"

"He gets that from everyone," Mom chuckles. "Come in, Tato. Make yourself at home. Dinner will be ready soon."

Dad hangs Grandpa's jacket in the closet and places his cap on the shelf. I lead Grandpa into the family room, and we sit on the couch. Dad changes the TV to the golf channel and sits on the single chair.

"You know, Tat, Marek is doing well in school," Dad says.

Grandpa leans forward. He wears a hearing aid. "What's that? he says."

"Marek is doing well in school," Dad says louder.

"Oh, that is great to hear." Grandpa looks at me and smiles. I smile back.

Grandpa turns his head and watches golf. He sits with his feet crossed and his hands between his thighs. His arched back doesn't touch the back of the couch. Dad fiddles with his thumbs.

Chapter 3: Family

"Do you like watching golf, Dziadek?" I ask.

"It's okay. I sometimes watch it at home."

The conversation ends there. I sit quietly beside Grandpa. Mom walks into the room. "Dinner is ready, everyone."

Dad and Grandpa take the ends of the table. Mom holds a camera. "Marek, Amanda, stand beside Dziadek, and I'll take some pictures."

Amanda and I huddle around Grandpa. Dad smiles, and his eyes glisten from across the table.

Mom takes three pictures. "Perfect. Now let's eat!"

Grandpa tucks his napkin into the neck of his sweater and loads one slice of meatloaf, two spoons of mashed potatoes and a piece of cauliflower onto his plate. He leans his head over his plate and struggles to cut his meatloaf. Rough hands and bruised fingernails show the effects of his days as a railroad mechanic.

Dad sits with his elbows on the table and scoffs down mashed potatoes. Grandpa chews with his head down.

"You know, Tato, Marek painted that picture of Pope John Paul behind me," Mom says.

Grandpa's head shoots up. "Wow. That is beautiful. When Peter was a little boy, he always sat by the fridge and drew cartoons. He would—"

"Tat, nobody wants to hear about that," Dad mumbles through a mouthful of food.

Mom peers over at Dad. "Piotrek, of course, we want to hear about it."

Amanda and I nod. Grandpa smiles. He looks at his food and swirls his mashed potatoes. Grandpa doesn't share any more memories.

The Visit

He grabs a piece of cauliflower by the stem and eats it with his head down. Spots of gravy cover his napkin, and a bit of cauliflower rests on the top corner of his lip. He finishes his meal and wipes his mouth with his napkin. He wipes off gravy from his chin with the palm of his hand.

"Would you like some dessert, Tato?" Mom asks. "I have cheesecake in the fridge."

"No, thank you, Margaret. I should get going. I have things to do at home. Thank you so much for a great dinner and for inviting me to your home."

Grandpa pushes his seat back, stands up, then reaches into his pocket. He pulls out two cheques.

"Marek and Amanda, these are for you." He hands Amanda one cheque and me the other.

Dad looks at the amounts—$3,000. Tears fill his eyes. "Tat, you don't have to do this. This is too much," he murmurs.

"No, no, those are for the kids," Grandpa says. "I have missed out on so much. This is the least I can do for them. Put the money in your bank accounts, kids."

"Thank you, Dziadek," I say and hug him.

"Thanks, Dziadek," Amanda says and hugs him, too.

Grandpa walks to the front door and slips on his loafers. Dad pulls Grandpa's coat and baseball cap out of the closet and hands them to him. Grandpa zips up his coat, bends the brim of his hat and places it on his head. Mom, Amanda and I take turns hugging Grandpa. Dad grabs the keys to the Mercedes and opens the front door. Grandpa smiles, turns, and walks out.

"I'll be back in a few hours," Dad says.

Put a Hole in It, Won't You

Emily Davidson

The oven clock blinks 8:13. We have to leave by 8:30.

"Have you guys eaten yet?" Mom yells from upstairs over the noise of her hairdryer.

"We're doing it right now," I screech from the kitchen.

Mom feels guilty leaving early. She teaches problem kids at Edenrose Public School. Mom stomps down the stairs and approves Eric's breakfast choice—Shreddies with sliced bananas and oatmeal crunch. She rolls her eyes at mine—Lucky Charms. Mom buys Lucky Charms because she likes them, too.

Mom moves through the kitchen and family room as she pulls rollers from her hair. She scatters them around the house.

"Have you guys seen my keys? Where are my car keys?" Mom barks at us in her get-a-move-on voice.

We transform into car-key searchers. Ten minutes later, the keys reveal themselves—on the hook where they belong.

Mom pulls on her brown jacket. "At least be civil with each other," she tells us.

Yeah, right.

At the breakfast bar, I sit next to Eric and spoon the last floating purple horseshoe marshmallow into my mouth. I study Eric's face. I hate his pointy nose. I hate his black clothes, and I hate his voice. Eric reminds me of cold, clammy feet. His eating habits make me shudder.

"Why can't you just stop breathing?" I ask.

"Why can't you just spill Super Glue on your face?" Eric crunches a mouthful of Shreddies.

"You disgust me," I say.

I elbow Eric during the cereal-eating moment of truth. The milk in Eric's spoon swishes. Some Shreddies make it to his mouth. The rest cascade onto his lap.

I point and giggle.

Eric's dark eyes examine the stain on his crotch, then look up and meet mine. I run. My long legs carry me swiftly up the stairs, but Eric stays at my heels. I slam the door to my room. Eric's fists pummel the other side. I lean hard against the door. My feet brace against a heavy dresser

"Ha!" I say. "You're such a loser."

Eric pounds with his fists. My muscles strain to hold the door shut. I hope he doesn't rip my horse pictures taped to the outside of my door.

The clock beside my bed blinks 8:22.

Silence ripples through the hallway. My heart pounds in my ears. "If you think pretending to be gone is gonna make me come out, it won't!"

"Em," Eric says softly. "Come out. Promise you won't tell?"

"Yeah, right, dorkus. I'm not that stupid!"

"Seriously, Em. I won't hurt you. Just come out and see this."

I open the door slightly, on red alert for a body slam. I squint one eye and peer through the tiny crack. Eric has his "oh-oh" face. I open the door. Eric points to a foot-sized hole in the centre of the door.

"Holy shit, dude. You are in so much trouble."

"Em, you can't tell Mom. Promise? Please?"

Chapter 3: Family

So this is what it feels like to play God.

"Look," I say. "I'll move the horse poster over the hole."

"Do you promise not to tell?"

"No, I won't tell. Pinky swear."

Eric and I peel the Scotch tape from the back of the horse calendar photos. We reposition all eight so that the new configuration looks natural.

At 8:45, Eric and I run to school.

～

Mom finds the hole in the door two years later.

Mariage d'Amour

Shelley Guo

I plop down on my piano stool and shuffle through the pile of sheet music in front of me. "Moonlight Sonata" by Beethoven, "Turkish March" by Mozart, "The Serenade" by Schubert, "Clair de Lune" by Debussy and "Grande Valse Brillante" by Chopin.

A loud thump in the living room distracts me.

Mom and Dad must be having one of their disagreements. Is it about the rent again? Or is it about something Alex or I did? I tiptoe to the door of my room and listen. No yelling or screaming. Yet. I turn the door knob slowly and edge the door shut. The door lets out a miserable creak before snapping shut with a loud click. I hold my breath, press against the door with my body, and pray that my parents don't investigate this awkwardly squeaking door. I listen for footsteps or movement in the living room. Nothing happens.

I sigh and return to the piano. I'm in the mood for some Beethoven. I pull out, "Für Elise."

I lock my fingers together, stretch my arms out, and push my palms outward. I rub my hands together to warm my fingers and wiggle and shake my hands to relax my arms.

I take a deep breath and lay my hands on the piano keys. I know "Für Elise" by heart, and the music flows from my fingertips. I'm in sync with the turns and dynamics of the music. I close my eyes, sway my body to the rhythm, and forget about the world around me. It's just me, the black and white keys and the sounds that come from me pressing them.

Chapter 3: Family

I near the end of the piece, but I stop in the middle. Sounds of shattering glass and screeching chairs come from upstairs.

My eyebrows knit together. I shut my eyes, try to push the noise out of my head, and get back to my music. But the racket prevails.

I sit still and listen to Mom and Dad conduct their orchestra of anger and hate. I make out foul words, desperate cries, heavy breathing and a ticking clock. A few moments later, BAM CRASH. I no longer hear the clock.

I hate when Mom and Dad fight—too much noise for me to play music.

I practice my scales and arpeggios.

I hear something, or someone, banging against the wall. I start with the A-minor scale. A chair tips over—I hope the chair is empty—and lands with a loud crash.

Mom's voice shrills an octave higher than my scales. She cries for help. She yells, "Madman!"

SLAP. THUD. WHAM. More cries from Mom.

I don't dare rush to the scene. The last time I tried to stop Dad's rage, I got a stinging red mark on my cheek and a pair of broken glasses. Dad doesn't like to be interrupted when he's "teaching a lesson."

My head droops low, and tears splash onto the black and white keys. I feel like a coward, hiding behind my piano when I know Mom hurts outside my door. I picture her woeful eyes and conflicted emotions when she tries to comfort me with a smile while tears and melted mascara run over her face. I wish I could open my door and take Mom into my room. I wish I could tell her how much I want to protect her.

I take out Richard Clayderman's "Mariage d'Amour." It's Mom's favourite piece. She says it reminds her of the first time Dad asked her out to a piano concert ten years ago.

For you, Mom.

Chapter 4: Relationships

Present a picture of a romantic relationship by detailing events you have experienced or observed.

Behind the Bushes

Bilaal Mohamed

My phone vibrates on the desk. My heart jumps. I grab my phone and see a new text message from Marisa.

"Meet me by the bushes at recess."

My vision blurs. My body trembles. My eyes dart to the clock above the chalkboard. Five more minutes until recess. The thumping in my chest drowns out my math teacher's voice. I scribble on my notebook, and pretend to pay attention. The chipped blue walls of my fifth-grade classroom close in on me.

I need to get out.

The bell rings, finally. I zip out of class and head into the nearest washroom.

Marisa and I have texted each other for months. What started as an accidental poke on Facebook over the summer snowballed into non-stop texts after school. Our relationship has brewed into something special. On January 11th we admitted we liked each other. On January 27th we held hands on school grounds. And today, on February 11th, we will have our first kiss.

Fuck. I feel nauseous.

I collapse onto the washroom sink, let out a few dry coughs, and catch my breath. My stomach rumbles. I look at myself in the mirror and examine every fibre of my blue button-up shirt, every cell on my nose, cheeks, forehead.

I turn on the tap and splash water on my face.

"OUCH, SHIT!" Hot water scorches my skin.

Chapter 4: Relationships

I check the mirror to see if my face has melted off. I dig a pick out of my pocket and use it to tug my afro. I huff into my hand and sniff my breath and recoil from the stench and pop two mints into my mouth, and throw in one more for good measure. I gloss my lips with Strawberry-flavoured Chapstick. I practice what the YouTube kissing tutorials taught me by puckering my lips and pressing them against my two fingers. I adjust my bright red tie and tuck in my shirt to look more professional.

I rush out of the washroom before my overthinking paralyzes me and wrestle through the crowd of students that march down the halls. I fly down the stairs and out to the schoolyard.

A small, lush garden, filled with bushes and sunflowers, lies at the far corner of the field. I speed-walk through the field, passing middle school students. Some play soccer, some eat their lunch, some lie down and soak in the sun. My friends, Angelo and Shaneil, stand with two of Marisa's friends. They wave at me.

Shaneil points toward the bushes and confirms that Marisa waits for me behind them.

I take a deep breath and face the tall bushes. My head turns back. Everyone gives me a thumbs up. I muster the courage to put my foot into the bushes and power my way through.

"Bilaal's probably gonna puke on her because he's gay," I overhear Shaneil mock me.

"Stop ruining their moment," one of Marisa's friends says.

I ignore their teasing. Those losers can't talk to girls without stuttering.

I reach my destination. Brambles and leaves cling to my clothes. Marisa stands on flat grassy ground. Sunflowers surround her. She wears a buttoned-up floral shirt with blue jeans and high heel boots.

Shiny, curly hair grazes her shoulders. Her tanned skin glows in the sunlight. My mouth hangs open like a cartoon character.

"Hey," Marisa says.

"H-hi."

"Are you ready?"

"I uhh I th-think I-I am." Her beauty makes my words tumble.

We giggle.

We lean into each other. I tilt my head too fast. Our foreheads clash against each other.

We giggle and start over.

Our lips press into each other, and the world slows. Ecstasy runs through my veins. I envision us ten years from now: drinking wine and cuddling after we put the kids to bed. Our lips disengage. We look at each other dumbfounded and then lower our heads out of shyness.

I dash back to the bushes because I don't want to make a fool out of myself in front of her. I glide past Angelo and Shaneil. I pity them for never having experienced a real kiss.

Yellow

Andrew Ihamaki

The soles of my sneakers chirp against the tiled gym floor as I manoeuvre around Jessica's toes. Speakers blast the song "Yellow" by Coldplay from a mixed CD. Overhead streamers stir with the weight of everyone's hot breath. The basketball nets catch the lights from the strobe. Boys and girls stand separated at each end of the court. Only Jessica and I, and three other couples, dance together.

The gym reeks of odour from the armpits of thirty twelve-year-old kids. Matt, Dan and Drew push and shove each other as they fight over who gets to dance with Jordan. Matt has Dan in a head-lock, and Drew throws in a punch whenever he sees an opening. They have been fighting over the girl all night.

I rotate Jessica in tight, timid circles and study everyone and everything around us. I examine every brick on the wall and search for a place to rest my eyes—anywhere but on Jessica. I settle on the wall over Jessica's right ear and follow the horizontal lines of mortar until they reach the doorframe of the fire escape.

I look down and smile awkwardly at Jessica, then nervously look back at the door.

Mrs. McCallum saunters past the bowl of lukewarm punch. She opens the fire escape door to alleviate some of the discomfort. The open door unveils a view of the sun setting over the hayfields outside. A soft breeze tickles the tips of Mrs. McCallum's short blonde hair. Her shawl catches flight, then drifts back to her shoulders. She grabs one of the vacant folding chairs that line the gym walls and props open the door. The outside air brings little relief.

Sweat seeps from my pores and beads slowly down my eyebrows and chin. My hands clam up as they hover over Jessica's waist. My stomach boils with nerves. My tongue goes numb. Words dribble out of my mouth like drool.

"You look so beautiful, Jessica," I say. We lock eyes. She just smiles.

"No, Jessica, you're so pretty, like, definitely the prettiest ever." She smiles again.

The clock on the wall reads 9:15. The foul air in the gym still hangs heavy, but Jessica smells sweet. Her hair smells like vanilla. Her neck smells like cinnamon.

I move closer and work up the nerve to look at Jessica again. A single lock of sandy blonde hair escapes her up-do. It falls to frame the left side of her face. Her skin glistens. We lock eyes again.

She smiles at me.

I love the way her smile makes her nose scrunch and squishes her freckles. My skin blisters with goosebumps. I want to kiss her so bad. I've had a crush on her since the first day of school. Now I tremble in a lake of cold sweat, unable to make a move. The song continues to pump through the gym as we dance. The lyrics of "Yellow" mark each gut-wrenching second and say every word I wish I could.

You know I love you so. You know I love you so.

I lean in. I pull back. Any normal person would kiss her.

"Is everything okay?" she asks.

I swallow the bag of marbles in my throat and stare into her eyes.

Chapter 4: Relationships

My heart runs laps as I work up the nerve to tell Jessica how I feel about her. I have so much to say. I want to tell her about the freckles on her nose, how she sometimes snorts when she laughs, and how I want to hold her hand every day at recess. I want to tell Jessica all the things I love about her. I wish I could just rip the lyrics from the speakers and hand her a profession of my love.

Instead, as my feet barely miss crushing her toes, I whisper, "I mean it, Jessica. You are, like, so pretty. Really, like, so pretty."

She smiles.

Sneaking Out

Juliver Ramirez

I hold my breath and listen for any signs of stirring within the house. I wait for five seconds. I hear nothing. I glance at the digital alarm clock—1:15 a.m. By now, everyone should be asleep. I can't wait around and confirm it, though. Kimberly waits for me.

I slink out of bed. I avoid turning on any lights. I arrange pillows to make it look like it's me under the covers. Even in the darkness, the decoy sucks. But it will have to do. I'll be back soon anyways.

I strip off my wife-beater and shorts. My hands pat through the drawers of my dresser for my black jogging pants. I pull my navy-blue hoodie from its hanger in the closet. I weave past the furniture in my room and locate the night table. I pocket the essentials—cell phone, keys—and ponder bringing my wallet. I feel like taking it with me, but debit and health cards during this venture would only be a hassle. I leave the wallet behind. I'll be fine. I'm only going to be out for an hour or so. No one will even know.

I take a last look at the clock from the doorway—1:19 a.m. I slowly and carefully close and lock my door.

I take the lightest steps possible down the hall. The floorboards still creak. I chew on my lip and pace myself down the stairs. I don't even try leaving through the front door. Instead, I pick up my shoes from the doormat and tiptoe to the kitchen. The sliding door makes far less noise than the front door. Still, I handle the lock with both hands. I muffle and absorb the clicking. I'm not free yet.

Chapter 4: Relationships

Crickets chirp in the backyard. My neighbours' houses seem lifeless without lights. Somehow, the darkness out here is not as scary as the darkness in my house.

The windows of my parents' room stand open above me. I can't run off just yet. I tiptoe across the wooden porch with my socks on. I reach the grass and put on my shoes. I scale the fence, break into a jog a street away from home, and check over my shoulder. I smile. I can make it to Kimberly's house, a thirty-minute walk, in twenty minutes by running. I text her updates every couple of minutes. She wants to know that I'm safe. But she also wants me to risk my life just to see her tonight.

When she texted me, "I need to see you tonight," I knew I had to do something to get her back. Our summer romance had turned sour.

I slow to a brisk walk when I see Kimberly's house. I wipe the sweat off my face with my sleeve. I lower my head to each of my armpits. I'm not surprised they smell, but I'm still annoyed. This meeting is supposed to be perfect.

I wait on Kimberly's driveway and try to slow my breathing. I text, "Hey, I'm outside."

A minute later, Kimberly strolls out. The security alarm beeps twice. The door closes with a thud. I grimace.

I walk up and hug her. Kimberly's hoodie smells just like her freshly-showered hair. I inhale her scent before she breaks from the hug. We sit side by side on her front steps for two hours. We don't say anything meaningful. Kimberly hides her hands in her sleeves and blows into them for warmth. I put my arm around her to keep her warm. She shrugs it off.

Kimberly scrolls through Twitter and text messages for most of the time. I just sit. I can't think of anything to say. A few raindrops dot the walkway. We climb into her mom's SUV because we can't go inside the house. The leather squeaks as we settle into the backseat. The silence contains us.

I finally spill out my thoughts. I tell her I don't want to lose her. I tell her my parents will get used to the idea of us, to just give them some more time. I tell her that I'm still trying. My voice quivers.

Kimberly stays quiet. She shakes her head and looks out the window. We sit for another hour.

"Look at me," I tell her. Kimberly's eyes look tired and sad. "Say something, please."

"Jules, I can't do this anymore. I get to see everyone whenever I want—Johnny, Martyna, Eunice. I can call them up at two in the morning, and they would come out and chill with me. I can do that with everyone—everyone except my own boyfriend. What is that? Like, seriously. I can't do this."

The sky greys outside. It's five-thirty a.m.

Tears well in my eyes. I don't meet Kimberly's gaze.

"Alright, good night," I mutter. I pull on the door handle and start towards home.

"Juliver!" Kimberly calls after me. "Stop. Please, just stop!"

I keep walking. Kimberly catches up to me and pulls at my arm. "I won't let you walk home like this. I'm giving you a ride. Come on." I don't want to look at her. I don't move. I wipe my tears with my sleeve so I can look into her eyes. Just for a moment.

"I'm okay, really," I tell her.

A morning jogger stares as he passes by.

Chapter 4: Relationships

The raindrops on the passenger side window transfix me. We stay quiet the whole ride home.

The Birthday

Samantha Ashenhurst

I wake up fully clothed. My head throbs. The taste of Smirnoff Ice and pepperoni pizza coats my dry mouth. The sun shines in my eyes through the slats of the white Venetian blinds. I drag my sore body to the edge of my bed and stand on shaky legs.

The clock reads nine a.m. It's official—my teenage years have come to an end.

I open my bedroom door a crack and listen to the house. Silence. The pressure on my bladder forces me to the washroom across the hall. I puke twice, relieving last night's party with every retch. I scrub my grainy teeth until they feel smooth and new. The mirror reflects my tired, makeup-stained face. I rinse my skin with cold water and choke down three Tylenol tablets.

I leave the washroom. I look at my sister Shawna's closed bedroom door. She's still asleep. The carpeted stairs groan softly as I descend to the main landing.

A scribbled note waits for me in the kitchen.

Happy birthday!
Went to Aunt Gwen's. See you this afternoon.
XO Mom and Dad.

Bottles and plastic cups litter the kitchen counter. I ignore them and pour a large glass of orange juice. I swallow the drink in five large gulps. My throat feels raw from smoking too much weed last night, and the juice soothes and burns.

Chapter 4: Relationships

I leave the empty glass in the already-full sink and sneak quietly down to the basement. Dark wood panelling covers the walls. The decrepit green carpet makes the room smell musty and stale. I find Mark asleep on our ratty, grey loveseat.

His cropped, greasy black hair sticks up in all directions. His mouth lets out a gentle snore. I muffle a giggle as I observe Mark's skinny body sprawled on the loveseat. One of his bony arms lies across his chest, and the other swings a few inches above the carpet. He wears a Melt Banana T-shirt and a pair of black shorts. The blanket tangles between his long, bare legs. His socked feet dangle over the edge of the loveseat.

I approach him quietly, intending to wake him with a kiss, then pause. Mark's white Nokia cellphone rests on the carpet next to the loveseat. A small light in the upper right-hand corner flashes blue, indicating an unread text message. I step away from his dozing body and wonder who sent him a message this early on a Sunday.

My body trembles when I realize I already know the answer.

My feet feel hot in my new moccasin slippers, a birthday gift from Mark. I stand in the dark basement rec room, quietly biting the polish off my fingernails. Mark still snores. My eyes dart from his face to his cell phone. I decide I need to know the truth.

I snatch up his phone and sit cross-legged on the floor next to the couch. Mark's eyes remain closed. He doesn't stir. I unlock his phone. One unread message. I exhale heavily and inhale sharply. His phone shakes in my trembling hands. I study his face and determine that he's definitely asleep. Opening his inbox, I check the message's sender.

Vicki.

Of course.

The Birthday

Vicki, Mark's new co-worker, who is such "a cool girl." Vicki, the one who Mark's gone out for drinks with most nights for the past month. Vicki, the one who just broke up with her long-term boyfriend. Vicki, the one who Mark hasn't yet let me meet.

The blue light blinks. My finger hovers over the Open button. I hesitate. Do I want to ruin my birthday? I look at Mark's sleeping form on the sofa next to me and reflect on the past three years. I remember, vaguely, when we used to talk about our future together. After a trip to Montreal last summer, we spoke of starting a life in a foreign city or travelling around Europe after my graduation. I'm not sure when or why those conversations stopped.

Lately, unanswered phone calls and ignored text messages have worried me, but Mark always has seemingly legitimate excuses. I try to recall if he explained being three hours late to the party last night, but I don't think I even asked. I didn't want to start a fight in front of my friends.

He sleeps. I bite my short nails. I open Vicki's message.

"Can I have you tonight?"

My face flushes and my eyes water. I clutch Mark's phone in my hand and grit my teeth. My heart beats faster. I struggle to steady my breathing.

I sit on the carpet. I reread Vicki's words. I consider replying to her, to ask if she knows about me at all, but decide against it. I study the message until the words blur together and lose all meaning.

I stand above my sleeping boyfriend and toss his phone, message open, at his chest. It lands on his rib cage and jolts him awake.

"I think you've gotta go."

Mark looks confused. He picks up his phone and studies the screen. His eyes widen as he stares at the text message.

Chapter 4: Relationships

"She's just kidding around," he sputters.

Mark tries to stand up but the blanket, still wrapped around his legs, causes him to stumble. "This isn't anything."

"I think you've gotta go," I say again. My palms sweat and my body shakes. My face feels hot. I stand at arm's length from him, hugging myself. "We can talk later. I really don't care. But right now, you have to go."

Mark nods, his face blank. He pulls a pair of black jeans over his shorts and grabs his black backpack. I walk him upstairs to the front porch, not bothering to remove my moccasins. A mourning dove coos in the distance as we stand and face each other. The sky is clear and blue. Across the street, Mr. Carson mows his lawn. My nose tickles and my eyes water at the smell of fresh-cut grass.

Mark hugs me, his thin arms wrapped loosely around my shoulders. I let him but leave my arms and hands dangling defiantly by my sides.

"Call me later," he says into my hair. "I mean, call me when you want to talk. This isn't what it looks like. I mean it." He pulls away and looks into my eyes. "Happy birthday."

Mark shuffles across the street to the bus stop, fumbling in his pocket for the fare. I walk back into the house and lock the door behind me. I yank off my moccasins and whip them into the front hall closet. I place my fingers on my throbbing temples and head to the kitchen. I grab an oversized garbage bag from under the sink and start cleaning.

The Summer Afternoon

Kael Reid

Lori and I ride our bikes through the forest, beside the Speed River, and out to Guelph Lake, a human-made reservoir on the edge of town. Dry pine needles lie like an orange carpet along the trail. Shafts of sunlight beam through the prickly lodge-pole pine boughs overhead. The air is humid, and the shade of the trees provides some relief from the July sun.

Our bike chains whir over metal sprockets. Twigs snap underneath our tires. We glide through occasional patches of wet mud.

Two men in shorts and tank tops stand in the middle of the trail ahead. I fall in behind Lori as we get closer. One of them gabs and gushes and gestures with one hand. We pedal past them.

Further down the trail, a couple of women with short, spiky haircuts and brightly-coloured running shoes walk briskly in our direction. We cycle by, and I catch a whiff of perfume.

The forest is quiet again. The Speed River winds alongside the muddy embankment. A duck stands at the edge of the river and quacks. We pedal alongside one another in silence for a few minutes. But I want to race. I pump my legs faster. My lungs heave as I zoom ahead.

"Hey!" she calls out from behind me. "You said you wanted to do a mellow ride!"

"I lied!" I yell. "C'mon, put those hockey quads to work!" I laugh.

Chapter 4: Relationships

I swerve around gnarled trees and manoeuvre over twisted roots. I splash through puddles and duck under low-hanging branches. "Wahoo!" I holler as I fly down a short hill. I crank my handlebars around a corner and keep pedalling. The forest opens up. The lake appears between the trees.

Lori's voice echoes through the forest. "You suck!"

I turn my head sideways to try and catch a glimpse of her. The trail looks empty. I squeeze the brake levers on my handlebars. My bike comes to a stop at the side of the trail. I put my feet on the ground and take the small backpack off my shoulders. I reach inside, pull out my water bottle, and unscrew the lid. I take a swig. My breathing slows. A robin warbles in the branches overhead. A squirrel prattles on a log. A warm breeze drifts over my bare arms.

Tires and pedals rotate closer and closer on the path behind me. I thrust the water bottle out to Lori as she approaches me. I jut my hip out and give her my cutest grin.

"Water break, sweetheart?"

Her feet push hard against the pedals. She grins and picks up speed. I see the bulge of muscle on her thighs. Man, I love those quads.

"Water's for losers!" she hollers and speeds past me.

"Damnit!" I jam the lid back on my bottle and stuff it into my backpack. I sling the backpack across my shoulders, get back on the seat and race to catch up.

When I arrive at our spot overlooking the lake, her bike leans against the trunk of a maple tree. She sprawls on the grass. I park my bike up against hers.

"Water break, sweetheart?" Lori holds out her water bottle. She smirks and raises her eyebrows at me. Why is she always so cute?

The Summer Afternoon

"You're a jerk!" I laugh and shake my head.

I flop down beside her and put my head on her stomach. Her shirt feels damp and warm. My head moves up and down as her chest expands and falls. I fish a bandana out of the pocket of my cut-offs and wipe sweat off my forehead. Lori tucks her hand into the waistband of my shorts. The wind picks up and floats across our sweaty bodies. Sweeping branches of the maple tree sway above us. Pale blue sky peeks between the fluttering leaves. We inhale together. We exhale.

"What kind of bird is that?" Lori asks as she points past my head towards the trunk of the maple tree. A tiny bird with blueish-grey wings, a caramel-coloured breast, and a black and white striped cap dances up and down the bark.

"Let me check my app!" I retrieve my phone from my pocket and swipe my finger across the screen. I click on the red square that says "Audubon Birds." I browse "birds by shape." I scroll through the list of "tree-clinging birds" and look at the tiny photos.

"It's a Red-breasted Nuthatch, right?" I show her the picture of a little bird on my phone. It has black and white stripes on its head, blueish-grey wings, and an orange-coloured chest.

"Looks like it. What does it sound like, I wonder?" she reaches over and taps the miniature label on the screen that says "songs." Up pops a list of different sounds to pick from. "Toots," "nasal squeaks," and "chattery outbursts" are some of the choices.

She clicks on "toots."

"Yak-yak-yak-yak-yak."

Lori and I look at each other and chuckle. I press it again.

"Yak-yak-yak-yak-yak!"

The nuthatch flits from over to a branch above our heads.

Chapter 4: Relationships

"Whoa! Look!" I point.

"I see!" Lori smiles. "Press it again!"

"Yak-yak-yak-yak-yak!"

The nuthatch bobs and skips back and forth along the branch. The bird chirps in response.

"She's singing back to your phone!"

"I know! It's so cool!"

I press "chattery outbursts." A series of trills and tweets erupt from the speaker. Another nuthatch darts from the leaves and lands above us. And another. And another. And another. They hop and jitter across the branches. Then, I press "nasal squeaks." Another nuthatch shoots past us and lands on the tree trunk. He shimmies up and down the bark and cocks his tiny head side to side. He clucks and peeps.

I jab Lori in the hip with my elbow. "There are so many!"

"This is incredible. I've never seen this before," she says.

"Me neither."

A nuthatch rockets down from above and dive-bombs Lori's head, and just misses her nose. It swoops back up into the branches.

"Whoa!" She shrieks and clenches her eyes shut. She laughs.

"Wow! Awesome!" I burst out. I grab her leg and laugh, too.

My heart feels like it's swirling and filling up with everything. Like it's filling up with all the little nuthatch songs—their chirrups and trills and cheeps. Like it's filling up with the warm wind and the golden late afternoon sunlight. Like it's filling up with Lori.

I reach back and brush her cheek with my fingertips. She wraps her fingers in mine and brings them to her lips. I roll over and take her body in my arms. We kiss. Her lips feel soft and warm. I rest my cheek on her collarbone. I breathe her in. She smells faintly of men's soap. The tiny birds twitter and frolic and serenade us from above.

Is this what joy feels like?

We disentangle and lie flat on our backs again. Our shoulders touch. We look up at the sky and watch clouds sail by. The nuthatches dart away, one by one. A crow caws from the top of a hydro pole over near the parking lot.

Lori turns to me. "Time for dinner?"

"Yeah," I say.

She rolls to her feet and reaches her hand down to help me up. She pulls my body to hers and looks at me.

"Can you feel how much I love you?" she asks.

Tears prickle under my eyelids.

"Yes." I hug her tightly.

We hop on our bikes and head home. We pedal back along the trail, side by side, along the river and the orange carpet of pine needles, through the trees and the shafts of sunlight.

Love Struck

Naomi Wilson

February 14th, Valentine's Day 11:15 am.

"Good morning my love," Tosen says. "Happy Valentine's Day!"

"Happy Valentine's Day to you too. Where did you go?" I say, heavy-eyed.

Tosen hands me a blindfold.

He takes my hand, and we walk from the bedroom to the kitchen.

"You can take the blindfold off now."

I slowly take it off. Flowers, cake, chocolate, balloons, gift boxes and teddy bears spread out before me. The biggest teddy bear holds a card in one paw and a tennis bracelet in its other.

"Thank you, Babe. This is amazing."

"I just wanted to show you how thankful I am for you."

We kiss.

We take a long nap, go to the Keg for dinner, and enjoy a dreamy ride. At Tosen's house, we get ready for bed. I go to wash my face. I throw my phone on the bed and head for the bathroom. I return, excited to cuddle.

His face looks stricken, like someone has just died. Fear runs through my veins.

"What's wrong? What happened?"

"I looked at the message on your phone," he snarls. "Explain this." He hands me the phone. The screen shows a text I had with my friend Chanel. In the text, I told Chanel about this guy I saw at a party and thought was hot.

"First of all, why are you searching through my phone?" I bite back. "We don't do that. I just wrote Chanel that message. I never approached that man, nor did I ever speak to him. You're overreacting."

"What . . . the . . . actual . . . fuck!"

"Do not swear at me. I did nothing wrong, Tosen. You're reading too much into this."

Something snaps behind his eyes. Is it anger, rage, frustration? In my two years of knowing Tosen, he had never reacted this way.

"Can you just calm down?" I ask. "Let's talk in the other room."

Tosen storms out of the bedroom, slams the door, and shouts, "You bitch, you whore, you stupid idiot, you fucking bastard!"

"I just wanted to talk, and this is what I get? I'm leaving."

I pack my bag and march to my car. I slide into the front seat and lock the doors. Tosen pulls at my car door.

"Let me in!" he pleads through the closed car window. "Can we talk?"

"Nah, I'm good. I will not be disrespected by somebody's son."

"I was wrong. I'm sorry. Just come back inside, and we can talk."

I undo my seatbelt and get out of the car. He takes my bag from me and walks me back inside. I sit on the bed, teary-eyed.

"So, are you going to explain yourself?"

I sit silent. Anger builds inside of me.

"So, are you going to explain yourself?"

I turn in the bed, lie down, and scroll through my phone.

Tosen pushes me.

"Don't put your fucking hands on me!"

"I'm talking to you!" he screams. "You fucking bitch-ass whore."

Chapter 4: Relationships

"That's it. I'm done with you!"

Tosen hurls himself on top of me, swiftly, almost elegantly.

Confusion cascades through me. I wasn't sure what was coming. This had never happened before.

Smash, Tosen's fist rams my cheekbone.

I gasp.

Smash, his fist lands square on my lip. I scream. Something tells me to protect my head. I block the next punch.

Smash, his fist hammers on my arms. Smash, smash, smash. It goes on and on.

Bruised and bloody, I scream, "Help me, HELPP!"

Smash, slap, smash. A new fast and aggressive combo. Hot tears stream down my face.

I can't get him off.

He screams as he hits. He rips my arms away from my head. He grasps my neck. I feel faint. I feel myself lose consciousness.

"Help," I whisper. "Please help."

Tosen looks into my eyes. I see something switch in his eyes—like a trance lifted.

He drops me.

I scramble to my feet, grab my bag and run.

Tosen blocks the door.

"Please let me go, please."

"I'm so sorry, baby," he cries. "It was the devil. I swear it was the devil."

I stammer, "No, please, please, just let me leave."

Tosen moves to the side. I sprint out the door. He chases. I streak to my car.

I lock the doors and start the engine.

He jumps on my hood and screams, "NO, PLEASE! I'M SORRY."

I honk the horn. I press the gas. The car jerks forward.

He rolls off the car. I speed off, covered in blood and bruises. Panic electrifies me.

I shake with fear, helplessness, confusion, and sorrow. I weep. I try to calm down. I don't know how to. Then it clicks. Call my sister, Vanessa.

"Vanessa, Vanessa," I gasp.

"Hello, Naomi?"

"Vanessa, help me! Please, Vanessa."

"Woah, what's wrong? Naomi, speak to me! What happened? Where are you?"

"Vanessa, I'm coming, please. He hit me. He attacked me. Vanessa, I'm coming."

"He did what! Oh hell, nah! Where is he? How far are you? Okay, come."

I drive thirty minutes from North York to Richmond Hill. It is still dark when I arrive.

The lamp outside Vanessa's house lights her face. She stands in the window. I pull into the driveway, put my car in park and run to Vanessa's arms. I cry. I feel his fist against my skin.

I cry at the sight of my blood. I cry because of my bruises. I cry about the two years of my life, wasted. I cry at broken trust and a busted lip. I cry in Vanessa's arms.

"Don't worry, baby girl. You are safe with me. He can't hurt you again." Vanessa kisses my forehead.

Call It Even

Sandali Vithanage

A line of loud teenagers forms along the long driveway of the suburban house on Tuxedo drive. Red plastic solo cups, empty cigarette cartons, and crumpled Smirnoff cans litter the freshly cut grass. The smell of vomit surrounds large bushes. Couples make out in the dark shadows. Loud rap music blares onto neighbouring houses.

I enter the house. The smell of sex, drugs, and alcohol fills my nostrils.

Strobe lights flash chaotically and the bass of the stereo blares throughout the house. Framed pictures of a happy family lie broken on the marble floor.

"CHUG! CHUG! CHUG! CHUG!" the group of teenagers scream towards a girl who chugs beer through a funnel near the entrance of the kitchen.

I move past the group and make my way toward the basement. I squeeze myself down the tightly packed stairway. The haze of marijuana and cigarette smoke fogs my vision as I descend.

I enter the basement. The LED lights shine a blue haze on the bodies that dance together in the centre of the room. I place my black coat on the pile of jackets on the pool table.

"Sandali, you're here!" My friend Mia spots me. I sigh. Finally, a familiar face. My shoulders bump against bodies as I make my way towards her.

"Fuck, you look amazing!" Mia screams over the booming rap. Her sweaty body presses against me. Her bright pink nails grab me a shot of alcohol from the messy counter. She raises her pierced eyebrow and holds the shot under my nose.

I throw my head back and take the shot of Fireball. The orange whiskey burns a trail down my throat to my chest. "Is Tyler here?" I ask. I look around the crowded room for his face.

"Fuck Tyler, forget about him. He treats you like shit!" Mia screams. She hands me another shot.

"Yeah, fuck him!" I grab the shot and down it.

Tyler is my best friend. It's been three weeks since he last spoke to me after I drunkenly confessed my feelings toward him.

The room floats after my tenth shot. I gaze at my surroundings and see blurry faces.

"Where the FUCK is the bathroom!" I scream. I stumble against a body.

"Shit, are you okay?" a familiar voice asks. I stiffen. Coarse hands grab my limp body. My eyes grow wide as I make out the blurred features of Tyler's face.

"Shit. FUCK!" I yell, stumble, and trip past him. I dodge into a dark storage closet. My body slams against furniture. "Fuck me. OW!" I groan and rub my elbow. I slam the door. My uneven nails run through my tangled, sweaty hair. My head throbs with the blaring bass that penetrates walls.

The closet door opens. Tyler's tall, broad figure looms in the doorway.

"Fuck off," I groan and look away.

"Sandali, can we talk?" Tyler mutters. He gently shuts the door.

Chapter 4: Relationships

"Oh, now you want to talk? Where were you three weeks ago, you piece of shit!" I yell and flail my arms at him.

"Where the fuck are the lights in this room?" Tyler says. He feels around for a light switch. He eventually gives up and turns on his phone flashlight.

"What the fuck is wrong with you? Why didn't you text me? Or call? Or do literally anything!" I yell. My face heats up with anger and betrayal.

"I needed time," Tyler says. His jaw clenches, eyebrows furrow, and small veins pop out on his forehead.

"You hurt me," I spit at him. My voice breaks. Tears form in the corners of my eyes. I let out a staggered breath. My teeth dig harshly into my lower lip.

Though he hurt me, though rage consumes my body, though I want to punch him square in the face, all I can think about is how much I miss my best friend.

"I needed time," Tyler says, his voice rises an octave. His once bright green eyes now look dark.

His nostrils flare, letting out a short breath. He fiddles with the silver Celtic dragon ring I gave him on his sixteenth birthday. His eyes dart between mine. His pupils dilate as he takes one step closer to me.

"Tyler, I need to go," I say. My stomach groans.

"Wait, what? No!" Tyler exclaims. He grabs my wrist.

"No, Tyler, I'm serious. I—" my sentence is cut short. I spill the contents of my stomach on Tyler's white Adidas shoes.

I drop my head against Tyler's stomach and grip his beige flannel shirt for balance. Sweat drips down my forehead as I continue to stain his white shoes and the expensive floor with liquid regret. I cough the last remains of fettuccine alfredo out of my mouth. Tyler groans in disgust. I slowly lift my body upright and wipe the vomit from the corners of my lips.

"Call it even?" I cough out.

A couple of days later, I show up at Tyler's house with a pair of new Adidas shoes. We make up.

Fate

Nadia Mohammad

Palestine's spring brings wild green grass and splashes of red poppies. Baba's white jasmine shrub carries her fragrance. The sun releases a warm and cosy light.

I sit on the windowsill and look outside from the fourth floor of Baba's house. This floor has two wide balconies, one room in the centre and a washroom with a dusty Jacuzzi. Late afternoon action busies the street beneath me. Skinny, chubby, white and brown barefoot boys kick soccer balls in the streets of my village, Al-Tira.

Mahmoud sings to me. His warm and loving voice rises from my phone and caresses my ears.

Mahmoud sings.

I lie down on the floral-patterned mat and close my eyes. I block out distractions. This is my scene, innocent and untainted.

Mahmoud sings the words of Egyptian poet Ahmed Fouad Nigm:

> *How could I ever regret our love?*
> *How could I ever find joy in your distance?*

Silence.

My chest rises and falls with every inhale and exhale.

This is my scene. I engrave this moment in my head. I want to remember each word, tone, breath, and heartbeat, no matter how this story ends.

"Nadia, are you there?" Mahmoud's voice ends the stillness.

"Bahebbak," I say.

"I love you too, habeebty."

"I wish I could hold your hand."

"Give me your hand."

"Here."

"I'm sitting next to you. I am gently touching your hand. It's so soft. Is that lavender-scented lotion?"

"No, it's vanilla," I smirk.

Mahmoud is my boyfriend. Well, I don't think I can call him my boyfriend. We've never been physically together. He's my potential husband—no, my partner—no, my lover.

Mahmoud, a Palestinian refugee, lives in Canada. Israeli soldiers bar Palestinian refugees from entering Palestine.

I, a Palestinian American citizen, live in Palestine. My father won't allow me to leave Palestine alone.

In 2004, Mahmoud and I met online. Mahmoud worked on his Master's of Architecture in Australia. I studied in my second year of undergrad at Birzeit University in the West Bank. Mahmoud and I have carried on a long-distance relationship for the last two years.

Mahmoud now prepares to travel to Chicago to ask my father for my hand in marriage.

"Are you ready?" I ask.

"I've been waiting for this moment for two years. I just hope your father likes me."

~~~

I sit up and hug my knees in my room. I stare at my phone. Outside, little thumbs flick marbles. My youngest brother, Suleiman, shouts at one of the neighbourhood boys, "It's not Ahmed's turn! It's Mazen's turn!"

Chapter 4: Relationships

The phone rings. "Hello?"

"Yes, habeebty," Mahmoud says.

"How was it?"

"It went well. I don't think there was chemistry between us. But he said he would study the matter with you and the family when he goes back to the West Bank."

The grey cloud in my head shrinks. I see our wedding day with my family and Mahmoud's family and we take pictures together and everyone smiles.

"That is great news!" I say.

"I know. It is happening, Nadia. Our dream is coming to life."

"Did you tell him how you met me?"

"Yeah. I told him that I first met you through a video conference, and then we worked together on several bridging projects."

"What do you think of my father?"

"He was very calm. Um, things got a little weird."

"What do you mean?"

"Well. He asked me for my ID."

"Your ID?"

"He didn't believe that I am a Canadian permanent resident. I think he thought I want to marry you for your American papers."

"Of course, he did. Did you show him your ID?"

"Yeah. I gave him my Canadian Permanent Resident card. He went through each line. Front and back." Mahmoud chuckles.

"I'm sorry you have to go through all of this."

"Don't worry, habeebty. It is all worth it in the end."

That night, my father calls. My mom says he wants to speak to me. My heart feels like it will jump out of my body. I tread to my parents' room. My mom hands me the phone. I try to decipher the expression stamped on my mom's face. Nothing. My trembling hand grips the phone.

"Hello."

"Who is this guy, Mahmoud?" Baba says calmly.

"I don't know him that much. We've worked together a couple of times."

"How do you talk to him?"

"We've sent each other emails about our project through the university. Our project is called Right 2 Education."

"I'm very disappointed in you," Baba hisses.

A shiver climbs up my back.

"I'm sorry, Yaba."

I give the phone to Mama.

He knows.

~~~

"Your father says if you or your sisters leave the house without the jilbab, he will divorce me," Mama tells me.

"I will never wear that tent," I say.

It's been two months since I graduated from university. I haven't left the house since. I refuse to step outside in a jilbab, the long loose Islamic garment some Muslim women wear as a sign of modesty, devotion, or in my case, control. I have covered my thick brown hair with the hijab for over ten years. I do not believe in it anymore. I do not want it to control me.

My mother knocks on my bedroom door. "Can I come in?"

She sits next to me on my bed. She sits close to me.

She sits too close to me.

Chapter 4: Relationships

"Nadia, I want you to be happy. I don't want you to suffer in your marriage the way I have. I want you to find a good husband. Please, Nadia. I want to see you out of this hell. This time it's different. This 'arees (suitor) is a nice guy. He is young, religious and open-minded, and he's blond and has blue eyes. Please, Nadia. Give it a try."

I listen to Mama. She has never spoken to me so softly before?

~~~

Rana, my younger sister, picks out a long pink skirt, a red long-sleeved shirt and a pink head scarf for me to wear. Rana and Yara, my youngest sister, cover my face with makeup.

We all go downstairs in procession. Lina, my older sister, prepares Arabic coffee in the kitchen. She uses the guests' cups. Gold colours the rim of the small ceramic white cups. Lina waits for the coffee to create foam on the surface. She pours the coffee and spoons the foam into the small cups. Lina gives me the tray, and Rana holds the living room door open.

The coffee's aroma and I slip into the living room.

I offer my mother coffee. I offer Miss Ibtihal coffee. I offer the 'arees coffee. I place the tray on the coffee table. I sit down. I look straight at the 'arees who sits across from me. My eyes scan him. I try to see what lingers inside him.

Is he a good watermelon or a bad one?

I don't know. Nobody knows. Is he like Bilal, my eldest sister, Dina's husband? Will I wake up one day on the floor with a pounding head, a blood-oozing ear and a bruised face while my two little girls stand over me?

Or maybe he is my father? Will he cause me to miscarry my first baby? He could be Lina's husband. He's a nice guy. He will let me work as a teacher. He will let me have girlfriends. He will let me wear makeup and perfume.

Miss Ibtihal, the 'arees's aunt and my former teacher, interrupts the tension. "Ahmed sings in the Islamic choir in America. He has a very nice voice."

I say nothing and look at him. My mother's face flushes.

I wait until it is suitable for me to leave the room.

The guests leave, and my mother barges into my room. "Your father wants you to marry him," she announces.

"I don't want to marry him."

"Your father says you will marry him whether you like it or not. He's coming back in two weeks."

One Week Later
"Hello? Mahmoud?"

"Hi, habeebty. Are you ready?"

"Yes."

"Be careful."

"Okay."

"I'll see you tomorrow."

"I love you."

"I love you," I reply.

I step outside the house in a black jilbab, a white head scarf, and a backpack. Boys play tag and girls play hopscotch on the street.

The sun watches over me as I make my escape.

Chapter 4: Relationships

It is 2022. The chill of Toronto's winter makes itself felt. It has been sixteen years since this city first took me in. Mahmoud, my husband, and Salam, our nine-year-old daughter, and Lamees, our eleven-year-old daughter, and I sit around the dining table and eat zahr blaban (cauliflower in an aromatic yogurt sauce) with rice in silence. I know the silence means everyone enjoys dinner. I want to bask in this moment of serenity and contentment.

I wonder if my family in Palestine has found peace.

I Love You, Too

Daniella Medel-Lawrence

"You know you mean everything to me, right?"

"I know."

"I'll miss you if you leave."

"I know."

"You're breaking my heart."

"I . . . I know."

"I can't imagine a world with you gone." My voice quivered. "Please don't leave."

Vincent stared at the night sky. Not a single star twinkled—it was only Vincent, me, and the empty roads of our neighbourhood littered with dry leaves and trash. Frost mushroomed up the skinny naked trees that lined the roads.

"I . . . " Vincent started only to close his mouth. The cool November wind blew between us, causing me to shiver in my thin sweater. Vincent only pulled his long sleeves further down his arms.

"Is there anything I can do to make you stay?" I asked. My nails dug into the soft skin on my palms.

"No, no, I don't think so." He sighed and broke the deafening silence.

"But what about all the memories, and our plans for the future? What about travelling and graduating together? What about finally getting your license and getting into uni?" I questioned, firing each of them after the other without taking a breath.

Chapter 4: Relationships

"You'll just have to do all of those things without me!" Warm tears streamed down his face. "You'll have to do everything without me. Life goes on, Daniella. Nothing will change when I'm gone."

"You're so mean."

"I know... I'm sorry." He sighed and looked down at his hands. Vincent fumbled with them, picking at the skin tags around his nails.

"My life will be different when you're gone. What if I don't want to do all the things we planned together by myself, huh? What then?" Tears ran down my cold cheeks and into my mouth. "Why are you doing this? Why don't you want to live anymore?"

"Because!" he yelled, whipping around to face me. "I can't do this anymore. I'm tired. I'm so fucking tired, Daniella. I'm not as strong as you."

I looked down and unclenched my fists. Crescent-shaped cuts lay in rows on my now bleeding palm. When I looked back up, Vincent still stared at me.

He was right. He did look tired.

He looked pale and hollow. His blue eyes were bloodshot and puffy from crying. Dark bags hung above his once bright eyes that looked at me with so much love, and his eyebrows seemed permanently furrowed. Soft pink lips were now chapped and bloodied from getting picked at, and his hood held down his unruly sandy blond hair.

"You have to try, Vin."

"Haven't I tried enough?"

"If you won't try, then how can I try?" I reached up to hold his cold face in my sweaty hands. "I wish you knew how much you mean to me."

The wind howled past us and the cold air bit at our noses. My breath clouded my vision, and the air stung my dry throat. After staring into each other's eyes for a few seconds, I pulled him into a tight hug.

He felt so familiar. Our bodies fit into each other. He smelled like rain and the shampoo that I left at his house.

A streetlight flicked down the road and then completely shut off. Darkness swallowed the sidewalk.

"I love you," Vincent said after a short pause. His voice shook almost as much as his shoulders.

"I love you, too." I cried.

~~~

A while after that night, Vincent started hanging out with a bad crowd at school. We got into an argument about how he was destroying his body and that I wanted what was best for him, but that was the last time we spoke. I asked one of my friends I went to high school with if they knew anything about Vincent. They told me that he had moved away after we graduated.

I don't know what happened to Vincent.

Jump

Emily Bonilla Rojas

A cold breeze sends chills down my back. I sit on a soft picnic blanket in the grassy field of Lisgar Community Park. The green from the leaves on the swaying branches fades into different pigments of yellow and orange. The sun still shines and soothes my chills from the wind.

Leo sits next to me and notices I'm growing cold. "Wanna go on a walk? It'll warm us up."

"Okay," I say and flash him a small smile.

He stands up, holds out a hand for me to grab, and helps me up. I bend down and grab the blanket we sat on and fold it neatly into the tote bag he brought. We walk to the nearest recycling bin and toss the now empty container of spicy California sushi we got from Metro.

We walk on a paved trail. People ride their bikes past and smile, and kids from the nearby middle school walk ahead of us. A large sign on the right of us reads Lisgar Meadow Brook Trail. Leo's eyes light up. He insists we walk through there.

We stroll along the trail, our fingers intertwined. At first, it was a clear path with surrounding trees. The path narrows as we walk and eventually disappears, and the space becomes tighter. We look ahead and contemplate turning around. Leo walks in front of me and pushes back the wild branches. He halts and I crash into him.

"What's wrong?" I ask.

"There's a lot of mud ahead. Are you sure you wanna keep going?"

Jump

"Yeah, I don't mind," I say. In fact, I do mind. But I know how much Leo loves going on walks.

The mud squelches underneath my shoes. I look down and frown.

"Leo," I say, "my new Nikes are gonna get ruined."

He looks down at my feet.

"I have an idea," he says. He turns around and squats. "Get on my back." He motions.

"W-What? Are you sure?"

"Trust me, Emily."

I take a deep breath and jump on his back. I cling to him, afraid of falling into the mud. My legs and arms tighten around him, and he grips the back of my thighs.

"Please don't drop me," I say.

He chuckles. "I could never."

He strides through the mud and thick branches until we see a quiet stream. The grassy field we sat on appears. Once the bushes clear up, Leo walks closer to the stream.

"Finally," he says, "we made it! We just gotta cross this stream, and up that little hill is our way out."

"But how do we get across? The water's filthy."

"We can just jump across it. It's not that big a jump."

"To you. You have long-ass legs. I don't."

"It's not even bad. Look," he says. He jumps across and lands on the other side.

I hesitate. He makes it look so easy, though. I can do it. I think. I take a deep breath and count in my head. One, two, three, go! I run to the edge to build up speed. But I halt. I can't do this.

"Come on. You got this!" Leo says, "I believe in you."

Chapter 4: Relationships

I once again step back and run. I get ready to jump and stop right before I do.

"Emily, you don't have to jump. It's okay, we can just walk back through the trail."

"NO. I am not walking all that again. I'd rather jump."

"Emily. Seriously, let's just walk back."

"No way."

"Fine," he says. He jumps back to my side and scoops me into his arms, bridal style. "I'll bring you to the other side."

"Leo, no. If you fall and get hurt, I won't be able to help you."

"Trust me, Emily."

I shut my eyes tightly. He readies to jump. I squeal. I feel him lift off the ground.

Leo slips. My butt hits the ground and makes a small splash. I'm too scared to open my eyes. I squint one eyelid open slowly until I meet Leo's eyes.

We look at each other blankly. We burst out laughing. I scan around us. I'm on the ground, and Leo's arm still holds onto me. He sprawls out on the ground in front of me. His shoes dip in the water. I stand up and dust off the back of my pants. I help Leo up and intertwine my fingers with his. We make our way up the hill.

"I never would have made that jump," I say.

He laughs and squeezes my hand, "I know."

Chapter 5: People

Use details of action, speech, and setting to present a person you know.

The Morning

Tara Monfaredi

I follow Brianna up the stairs from Comfort Zone, the notorious after-hours club tucked away in the basement of the Waverly Hotel. She swings the door open. Her cloudy curls block out most of the daylight. The early morning sunlight stings my eyes as I step onto the sidewalk at the corner of College Street and Spadina Avenue. I wince, rub my eyes, and pull my phone from my pocket to check the time.

"Oh my God," I groan. "How is it seven o'clock already?"

"Fuck, right?" Brianna says.

The dark, windowless Comfort Zone has a casino effect on time. Dance music blares, coloured lights flash, and people high on uppers do the shuffle for hours. I can't dance and I don't like dance music but this is where I've spent the last four hours, dancing to dance music, high on uppers. My jaw feels tight and sore. My limbs feel heavy. A tinnitus ring pierces my eardrums.

"What are we saying now?" Brianna asks.

"I dunno. Daria's texting me about the movie. I have the tickets."

"What movie is it?"

"I don't even know . . . it's French. Let me check." My sister, Daria, and I volunteer for the Toronto International Film Festival. The Festival organizers compensate us with vouchers we redeem for movie tickets. Daria already traded the vouchers for tickets earlier in the week and gave them to me to hold onto. I look through my purse and find them tucked away in a pocket.

Chapter 5: People

"It's called *L'Ombre des Femmes* (*In the Shadow of Women*)," I tell Brianna.

Brianna and I both speak French. We attended Bramalea Secondary School as French Immersion students. We met in ninth-grade French class ten years ago.

"Daria wants us to go together 'cause she doesn't think she'll make it downtown in time anymore."

"Okay, sounds good," Brianna says. "I'm down."

A man limps over to us. Deep, vertical, jagged scars mark his face. His head is shaved. His clothes hang loosely from his body.

"Hey, can I bum a cigarette?"

A blonde woman stands a few paces away from us, waiting for him.

"Uhh." I open my pack and look down at the lone cigarette.

He leans towards me and peers in. "Just gimme the tip of it."

"Ah, batch for your spliff?"

I go to break off a few centimetres of cigarette from the top.

"Wait, wait, wait." He negotiates for another few centimetres. I comply.

He limps away. "Fucking guy," I mutter.

A few minutes pass before Brianna digs through her purse and pats her pockets.

"Whatcha looking for?"

"My phone. I just had it!"

"It must be somewhere! Just relax and look through your stuff again."

She pulls out her wallet, two pens, a small, clear bag of weed, a knit hat, a phone charger, a tube of lipstick, and a rolled-up server's apron from her bag before stuffing it all back.

"It's not here, Tara. My brand-new iPhone. I'm not buying a new one! I just got it."

"Okay, hold on."

I pull out my phone and hand it to her.

She puts my password in and opens a phone tracking app. A blinking dot appears on the map—the app detects her phone on the move.

"Any money it was that guy!"

"How though . . . ?!"

"I don't know, but let's go!"

We follow the mapped route to Toronto Housing at Dundas Street and Spadina Avenue.

We reach the blinking dot on the map, pass through the opening of the gate, walk through the small courtyard, and stop on the path in front of a row of townhouses.

"HEY! I KNOW MY PHONE IS HERE! I KNOW YOU HAVE IT!" Brianna yells at the houses. Her voice booms and bounces off the buildings in the silent complex. Wings flutter. A flock of sparrows vacate a nearby tree.

No answer.

"HELLO? I KNOW YOU HAVE MY PHONE! I KNOW IT'S HERE!"

No answer.

"I KNOW YOU'RE THERE, FUCKING ASSHOLE! I KNOW YOU CAN HEAR ME!"

No answer.

"I'M CALLING THE COPS! DO YOU HEAR ME? I'M GOING TO CALL THE FUCKING POLICE!"

"Oh my God, no, you're not," I say. She shoots me a look.

Chapter 5: People

"HELLO? I'M NOT FUCKING AROUND!"

A shuffling comes from inside one of the houses, the sound of a window closing.

"Did you hear that?" Brianna asks.

I nod.

The man appears from behind the row of townhomes, strolls around the corner, and saunters across the courtyard. He doesn't look at us.

"That's him," she says. "That's the guy!"

We beeline towards him. I stand beside Brianna a few paces back.

"Hey, where's my phone?" Brianna asks him.

"I don't know," he shrugs.

"I know you have it."

"Are you calling me a thief?" Anger washes over his scarred-up face. He furrows his brow and scowls.

"You did steal my phone, so . . . " Brianna stands tall, unafraid.

"Listen, bitch," he says. He steps toward Brianna. "Do you know who I am? Do you know what I could do to you?"

I step forward and inch between them. "Don't talk to her like that!"

My heart pummels my chest.

Her eyes lock on his.

"I don't give a fuck who you are. I just want my phone back." Her voice stays steady.

"You don't know who you're talking to, little girl. I could shoot you."

She holds his gaze and steps forward. Their faces almost touch.

"Do it then."

The Morning

At nine years old, Brianna lost her father, Robert, to gun violence. He was the fifty-first Toronto homicide of 2001. His file remains a cold case. At 2:37 a.m., close to Jane and Sheppard, on Kanarick Crescent, a seven-minute drive from where I live now, Robert suffered multiple gunshot wounds. He died in the hospital the following day, on October 20th. He was thirty years old.

Brianna turns to me and puts a soft hand on my arm. "I'm fine. Let me talk to him."

The calm of her voice reassures me. I step back.

"Where is it?" she presses.

"I don't have it, but I did see some guys back there." He throws his chin over his shoulder. "Maybe I can check for you," he says.

"Nah, you have it."

I pace the courtyard but keep my eyes on Brianna.

"If you're going to disrespect me, accuse me of something, I'm going to walk away," he says. "But if you say you know I didn't take it, and apologize, I'll take fifty dollars and do you the favour of asking those guys if they've seen it."

"If I get my phone, I'll give you fifty dollars."

"Show me the money."

She pulls her wallet from her bag and pulls out a fifty-dollar bill, lets him see it, then closes the bill in her fist.

"So?"

He turns around, takes two steps, digs in his pocket and turns back around, holding her phone. He waits for Brianna to open her fist and stretch out her hand, but she doesn't. Not yet.

"Okay, give it to me."

"Give me the money."

"You can have it after I have my phone in hand."

Chapter 5: People

"Gimme the cash first."

"Okay, at the same time," Brianna says.

He lifts his hand and holds up Brianna's phone. She lifts her opposite hand. Their arms hover between them for a second at stomach level. She snatches her phone from his hand as he snatches the bill.

She swings her body towards me. "Let's get outta here!"

We hustle through the courtyard to the sidewalk. We don't look back.

"Oh my God, Brianna!" I laugh. "I'm glad you got your phone back, but holy fuck! What if he killed you over a phone?" My heart still pounds.

Brianna laughs maniacally. "Fuck that shit. I wasn't going to let him get away with that. Plus, he wasn't going to shoot me. Fuck him! Still wanna catch that movie?"

"Let's go."

We head southbound on the Spadina streetcar to King Street, then across King to the TIFF Bell Lightbox.

We boot it to the third floor, to Cinema Three.

The black-and-white film, *L'Ombre des Femmes*, plays on the screen. The main characters, Manon and Pierre, navigate desire, infidelity, jealousy, passion, lust, and illusions of love.

Brianna's eyelids flutter and get heavier and heavier in the dark theatre. Her chin droops to her chest, and her head falls to the side. I fight off sleep for the next hour before my eyes get impossibly heavy, and I too knock out. I wake up to the cinema thinning out and the credits rolling. I put my hand on Brianna's shoulder.

"Brianna." I slump down and level my head to her slouched body. "Brianna."

The Morning

She shakes herself awake and sits up in the theatre seat.

"Hm?"

"Let's go," I whisper.

ESSE Lights

Hijin Baasandorj

"Psst," my cousin, Temu, whispers. "Let's go outside to the gazebo." He grabs his red leather jacket and hurries out of my room. We tiptoe around my parents' bedroom door and sneak down the wooden stairs of our summer house in Sharga Morit, a resort house district in Ulaanbaatar, Mongolia.

"Shh, you'll wake them up!" he mutters.

We step outside. My face soaks up the humid air. Crickets chirp among the bushes. Moths circle the only lamp that lights all the grass between our house and Temu's.

Of my twenty or so cousins, Temu was the only one I spent my childhood with. When we were little, our parents forced us to spend time together since we were only four months apart. Now we're best friends.

"I have something to tell you." Temu grabs my hand. We walk through the woods in search of our grandfather's old gazebo.

It's strange how all our houses are aligned in this heavily-wooded field with only one gate. Everybody from our Big Uncle to my dad to my Young Uncle has their houses here. It is my grandfather's dream that his nine children summer together within the same khashaa (fence). We've spent our summers together for the past fifteen years.

Temu walks with my hand in his hand in the pitch dark. I wonder why he grabbed his leather jacket when it's thirty degrees outside.

His white tank top clings to his skinny body. The leather jacket drapes across his arms.

"Okay, how do you turn the light on in this thing?" He stomps onto the steps of Grandpa's gazebo. I prance down to the switch and turn the light on.

"Your parents won't be able to hear us from here," Temu grins.

Temu takes his leather jacket onto his lap and digs through all of its pockets.

"Ah! Here it is." He fishes out a cigarette pack. They're the white skinny cigarettes that people say only girls smoke, ESSE lights. He throws his jacket to the side.

"We're eighteen now, Temu. You really think my parents would be mad at you for smoking?" I chuckle.

Temu sighs with a cigarette between his lips and offers me one. I shake my head.

"Of course, they'll be mad. Their own daughter refuses to smoke! At least try it once, Enkhjeen," he laughs.

Temu falls silent. Crickets chirp. "I don't know why I hid it in my jacket. It was just out of habit. Don't want to worry Mom, you know."

I sit next to him and hope the smoke doesn't come my way. It gives me numbing headaches. I think about Temu's mom, a sweet lady.

"You seen your dad in a while?" I look up at his face. Temu stares into the bushes in the dark. The ash at the end of his cigarette look as though they will fall. I point to his finger and gesture by tapping on the seat. He shakes his head out of a daze, sucks in the air, and taps off the ashes.

Chapter 5: People

"Nah. He's off living with his secret second family now." He grits his teeth. "Probably forgot about me and Ma by now anyways." Temu drops his ESSE cigarette and tramples it with his heel. I look at my feet. I heard about this from Dad earlier this summer. Temu's dad has two separate families with children on opposite sides of town. He had been deceiving us all. He's the worst.

"When's your mom coming?" I ask. Temu had been sleeping at our house for the past two days.

"She's not. I'll go downtown tomorrow at noon by myself."

I forgot that Temu can drive now. Driving is too scary for me. I look down at the pink floral patterns of my nightgown. Temu seems more mature, even though we're the same age.

"Enkhjeen," he lights up another one.

"Yeah?" Crickets chirp.

"I'm gay."

I turn to him. His hands tremble. He stares into the void beyond the bushes. His eyes water. His crossed leg fidgets.

"I know." I smile at him.

I hug him. He hugs me back. He sobs.

Buried the Jewish Way

Natasha Segal

We don't have ten men for the minyan. So we opt out of a synagogue service. Rabbi Zaltzman says he will try and get some people he knows to come and help carry the casket. A Jew needs ten men to carry his casket. Dyedushka didn't have ten male friends left.

We prop Babushka on a bench inside the cemetery. She can't make the long walk to the grave. As the small procession of old ladies from the building gathers around the open hole that awaits Dyedushka's body, Babushka sits and faces the sun alone.

The hearse arrives. The men who carry Dyedushka's casket barely know him; old men from his building, tricked into the job by friendly old ladies from down the hall. Their legs wobble, bow shaped, their shoulders sag beneath the casket's solid weight. Sweat pours off their wrinkled foreheads and stains the collars of their wrinkled shirts. They grit their dentures, smile strong smiles for the half-blind old ladies, and grip the edges of the plain pine box.

"Can I help?" I ask Rabbi Zaltzman.

"No, no." He waves me away.

I follow the old men's grunts down the hill to the hole. Three rabbis arrive. I only know Rabbi Zaltzman. I stand silent in front of the small crowd. Mama stands beside me. Behind us, the ladies of 3638 Bathurst Street fiddle with flowers and hairpins and hats. The rabbis wince at the flowers. Jews don't bring flowers to funerals.

Chapter 5: People

Rabbi Zaltzman leans on a gravestone. His black eyes scan the scant congregation. His beard has grown grey since we first met. The rabbi wears a black hat, a long black coat, shiny black shoes, black pants and a black shirt. All black, all the time. A Chasid—a strict Orthodox Jew.

"I have known Mikhail, Misha since I was . . . " Rabbi Zaltzman pats a spot beside his hip. "He always reminded me that we came from the same little village in Russia. Always when I saw him I would say, 'Misha, how are you today?' and he always smiled, always smiled and said, 'Very well. I am very well!' And that is how I remember Mikhail. He was always joyful and happy to see you."

A lump forms in my throat. My vision blurs.

Rabbi Zaltzman calls Mama. She stumbles over a patch of green grass and reaches the front.

"What can I say? He was a good father—the best, the best father   I am sorry   I cannot say anymore."

Rabbi Zaltzman extends his open hand to me. I look into his eyes and shake my head.

"Say something for your grandfather," he says.

Again, I shake my head.

"Are you sure?" the rabbi says.

I nod.

~~~

I called Rabbi Zaltzman yesterday morning.

"I need to speak to Rabbi Zaltzman right now," I told his secretary.

"He is a busy man. Can I take a message?"

"I need him now," I said.

"May I ask what this is about?"

"My grandfather just died."

"Oh . . . oh my, of course. I will go and tell him." She left me in the dead call-waiting air.

"Natasha," Rabbi Zaltzman's familiar voice, calm and slow, came over the telephone line.

"Dyedushka umer," I stammered. "Dyedushka died." The Russian word for "grandfather" rolled from my throat, broken between sobs, jolted on half-forgotten words. "He was a father to me, he raised me—Rabbi, I don't know what to do."

"You are in charge of the arrangements?" Rabbi Zaltzman asks.

"I guess."

"Will your mother be helping?"

"I don't know."

"Do you want me to call her?"

"I want to bury him the Jewish way."

"Of course," Rabbi Zaltzman replied. "We will handle everything."

Silence.

"What hospital is he in?"

"Sunnybrook."

"I will send someone there right now."

I leaned over my kitchen counter and wretched. My breath stopped. My eyes burned.

"Thank you," I croaked.

"Yes," Rabbi Zaltzman said. "Jews must be buried as soon as possible. We will bury him tomorrow. I will call your mother."

Chapter 5: People

Today, frail old men shovel brown dirt over a casket that sits snugly down inside the hole. The women watch. The rabbis pray. The crowd throws handfuls of grey rocks and soil into the wound. I grab a shovel. I shovel great shovelfuls of dirt into the grave.

"Who are you?" hollers some old man behind me. "Did you know him?"

"I'm his granddaughter," I say over my shoulder.

"Women aren't allowed to shovel dirt into the grave—we're Jews here."

I turn and hand him the shovel. He touches my shovel and then lets it fall to the ground.

"You useless fucking motherfucker!" I scream. The crowd freezes. "You want me to throw you into the fucking grave, too, you piece of shit, you bastard? You wanna see who's the real man around here, you want me to fucking show you?"

I strip off my shawl.

"I'll kill you, you useless fucking pig. Who the fuck invited you here! Who am I? Who the fuck am I? You want me to show you who the fuck I am?" I shake. My face burns. "Come closer, bitch! Come closer so we can show everyone who the fuck the real man is—you fuck, you useless, stupid old fuck!"

"Natashinka." Mama's fingers flutter over my shoulder. "Your babushka is all alone on the bench. You should go and keep her company."

"Fuck you, you bitch!" I spit. "You go and keep her company."

The old man looks to Rabbi Zaltzman. "I'm just an old man at a funeral," he chokes.

"Soon, it'll be your fucking funeral!" I say. "Learn to shut the fuck up before I shut you the fuck up."

"I'm just a man at a funeral."

"You're just a fucking piece of shit, is what you are."

~~

Yesterday afternoon I arrived at the intensive care ward at the same time as Mama and Babushka. The nurse looked at me quizzically as I barged through the hospital doors.

"She is my daughter, Mikhail's granddaughter," Mama said. "She is with us."

We marched to bed number thirteen. We formed a half-moon around Dyedushka's feet. Without his teeth, he didn't look like Dyedushka. A nurse slipped through two closed hospital curtains. She talked—fast—into Mama's ear.

"Explain to her," Mama pointed at me. "We do not understand your English."

I stood up, straightened myself, and faced the nurse, forcing myself to make eye contact. The nurse stumbled backwards through the curtains and mumbled something. I pulled a footstool beside Babushka's chair and sat by her swollen feet.

A rabbi came by.

"Ms. Sigalov? I am here from the funeral home. Rabbi Zaltzman sent me. I will make sure that everything goes by the Jewish rules with the body."

The body.

"They have already done more than we allow, according to the Jewish laws," he said and tilted his head. We nodded.

"I will perform some initial prayers now." The rabbi pulled out a small black siddur from a blue velvet pouch. He opened the book, then sauntered to the corner of our makeshift room and stood by

Chapter 5: People

Dyedushka's head, the sun to his back. He prayed in Hebrew, a short, melodious chant. He chanted us into a new world, a world without Dyedushka. He said "amen" when he was done, but it wasn't in unison with ours.

Then the rabbi wheeled Dyedushka's bed toward the curtain.

"I will take him and wash him and pray over him and bring him to the funeral site tomorrow," he said. Babushka nodded.

The rabbi told us it was time to go. We rose, gathered our things, and left.

An Old Jamaican Man

Janéa Achioso

Every Sunday after church, I go to see the Old Jamaican Man. I call him Grandpapa. I like the name Grandpapa because it is friendly and fun and feels secure and sturdy.

His light, warm, lovely smile turns a sour day sweet. I love his baritone, raspy Jamaican accent and his sweet songs. Grandpapa is like no other.

"Where are mi grandbabies, dem?" his grating voice booms.

"Grandpapa, Grandpapa! I missed you."

"Oh ha ha ha," he chuckles. "Come give mi mi hug."

I lean in and wrap my arms around him. He returns the motion with a slight squeeze.

"Your head is big like any man bread," he jesters. We share a laugh.

"Grandpapa, you always make that joke. What's a 'man bread' anyways?"

His laugh fills the four walls we sit in. His muscles pull his face into a smile. The laugh lines crease his forehead, and his eyes almost close as he guffaws.

"Boy, mi can suspect your age with that question," he cackles. "Jackfruit, a man bread is jackfruit."

"If my head is big as any 'man bread,' your head is big as any coconut then!" I mock his accent.

Grandpapa is funny, witty and crafty. He always knows how to make me laugh, even if the joke isn't funny.

Chapter 5: People

"You hungry? Should I make some mash-up potatoes?"

I giggle. "Grandpapa, they are called mashed potatoes. Can we go to McDonald's instead?"

"What do you know about McDonald's? You hafi McDonald's money?"

"I have Grandpapa money." I give him a sweet smile.

"You fi mek mi a popper," again he chuckles.

Popper is Grandpapa's way of saying I would make him a poor old man because he always spoils me.

He grabs his keys, and we drive to McDonald's.

"Order anything you want mi dear and get mi what you eat."

We sit in Grandpapa's car. He eats his junior chicken and medium fries. We share a 10-piece McNuggets. His hand slowly reaches for the radio. The monitor flips between stations before it lands on his favourite: 93.7FM, 70s classic reggae vibes. He eats and hums the radio songs and taps his thumb on the steering wheel. He radiates happiness. He feels content with his granddaughter, eating McDonald's in a FreshCo parking lot, listening to 70s reggae. It feels like this every time Grandpapa and I hang out.

"Grandpapa, what's your favourite song?"

"You can never go wrong with some Temptations 'My Girl.'"

I know what to do. I push my seat back and rummage to find the aux cord buried in the back seat. I plug the cable into the aux jack and connect it to my phone. I open Apple music and type in "My Girl" by The Temptations. I look at Grandpapa's face as I press play on my phone. There it is. That sweet smile.

"OUUUU WEE, turn up the song," he says.

I reach to turn the knob for the volume, but he beats me to it. The music plays full blast. Grandpa and I sing along.

An Old Jamaican Man

We harmonize.

I've got sunshine on a cloudy day.
When it's cold outside
I've got the month of May.

We jump out of the car. I dance and sing and watch Grandpapa's body shake with each laugh. I twirl, leap, prance, and cartwheel to the music. Grandpapa opens all the doors. The music blasts. We dance.

Grandpapa does his old man side shuffle, snaps his fingers on the beat, and his accent creates a rhythmic remix. We bellow.

I guess you'd say,
What can make me feel this way?

Grandpapa points at me and sings:

My girl, my girl, my girl

He takes my hand and spins me.

Talkin' bout my girl. My girl.

Just Grandpa, The Temptations, and me jam out in the FreshCo parking lot. The song ends. We laugh till our bellies hurt and make our way home, still humming "My Girl."

"Thank you, Grandpapa, for the McDonald's."

"Anytime mi dear," he smirks. "That's mi job to be a popper."

"Don't worry, Grandpapa. When I'm older, you can make me a popper, or whatever they call a rich old woman, because I'll never go broke."

There it is again, that sweet smile. I feel my mouth shape into a smile. He doesn't laugh at my comment. He beams at me. I ponder what his gaze means. He wraps his arms around me. They feel like a warm blanket. I hug Grandpapa back.

Chapter 5: People

"You children really mek mi life worth living."

My eyes fill with tears.

"What would I do without mi grandbabies? Twenty-one of yous. I couldn't be more proud."

From his arms, I look up.

Tears trickle down Grandpapa's face and get lost somewhere in his bearded smile.

Bill and Mr. Ram

Selina Africaine

A small crowd gathers around Mr. Ram, the headmaster, and Bill, my brother, in the sixth standard classroom. Bill, my sister Janet, and I attend St. Pius Roman Catholic School in Georgetown, Guyana.

Mr. Ram and I hate each other. I don't know when the animosity began. I know that he hates me and wants me out of his school, and I hate him, and I wish he would kick me out.

At home, Bill and I don't get along. He wants to be big and hates that I'm a year older than him. I just turned ten, and Bill nine. But outside the confines of our home, I protect Bill. I fight for him, and he fights for me. We have our own friends and hardly play together, but we support each other.

I enter the open doorway. Fear marks Bill's face. His bloodshot eyes fill with unshed tears. Rage darkens Mr. Ram's face. His nostrils flare, and oily sweat drips down his forehead from his greasy straight hair. His new cane will soon be in his hand and landing on Bill's backside.

I'm convinced Mr. Ram, a short, dark-skinned East Indian, hates all the Black students at St. Pius. Every Black child who ever got into trouble knows how cruel the headmaster can be. Once in a while, a furious Black parent comes to the school, aiming to do to Mr. Ram what he did to their child. Each time, we all gather around expecting to see Mr. Ram get his due, but he can be as slippery as an eel. He greets the parent with warmth and shows such care for

Chapter 5: People

the welfare of their kid. He talks about how he wants what's best for their child, and that's why he must be strict. The parent leaves the meeting angry with their kid and apologizes to Mr. Ram.

~~~

Students gather around Bill and Mr. Ram with fear and excitement on their faces. I stand at the fringe of the crowd, afraid to get closer in case Mr. Ram sees me. I have never seen Bill look so scared. I know he doesn't want to cry in front of all the students. He looks trapped, the headmaster determined.

"Bend over!" Mr. Ram speaks softly, yet somehow his voice booms in the hushed silence.

"Please, sir." The words just pop out. "Please don't beat Bill. Last night he had a fever."

Mr. Ram turns towards me. His face darkens. Two veins pulse on his oily forehead. His lizard-like yellow eyes fix on me.

"What did you say?"

"Bill, sir." My lisp worsens, and my tongue feels heavy. "He had a fever last night."

"Come here!"

I look at Bill as I move forward. He wipes away the tears that have spilled down his cheeks.

"Please, sir. I'll take Bill's licks for him." I force the words out of my dry mouth. "He won't do it again."

Mr. Ram looks at me. He seems amused and even smiles. "Okay, Mary. Bend over."

I bend over the desk and hold my skirt close to me.

"One."

Oh, God! The lash hurts more than any he has given me before, as if the cane cuts through the flesh to my bone.

"Two."

Sweet Jesus, I can't take it. Hot pee runs down my legs.

"Three."

Screams pour from my mouth. When I think I can bear it no longer and will faint, the lashes stop.

"Get out!" Mr. Ram orders. "Get out!"

I straighten up from the desk. My body trembles all over.

"Bend over!"

A gasp escapes from everyone's mouth. I stop and turn around. Bill bends over the desk. Mr. Ram's hand reaches high in the air. The cane gleams.

I feel hatred, blind hatred. I taste bile rising to my throat. I feel helpless, devastated, defeated, overwhelmed, and worthless. I turn and walk out of the room towards the front doors of St. Pius. As I step down the stairs, I see the green sugarcane fields in the distance. I wish I could lose myself there, where no one will ever find me.

~~~

Years later, I'm a new immigrant in Canada. I apply for a course in nursing. I need a recommendation from my old school. I write Mr. Ram. I hope he has forgotten me and will write a recommendation for a faceless past student.

Mr. Ram's reply comes promptly. I feel excited as I tear open the envelope. I picture myself in a nurse's uniform. I imagine my mother's face when I write and tell her I have been accepted to nursing school.

Chapter 5: People

> *To whom it may concern,*
> *I cannot in good conscience recommend Mary to a fine profession like nursing. She is the most difficult student I have ever encountered in my years of teaching. She was an undisciplined troublemaker, a cantankerous and vicious child, a child, who—*

The letter drops out of my trembling hands. Sobs shake my body. I feel as hopeless, useless and worthless as when Mr. Ram beat me as a child. I sit on the floor and cry. I cry until I can cry no more.

Then I tear up the letter and the application form for nursing college.

Diamond Heights

Rachel Smith

"I've come to take you. I've come to take you."

I sing the words like a ghost as I take my 101-year-old grandmother's hands and pull her arms gently toward me.

"I should stand up, but . . ."

I bend down and position her feet. We prepare for the ascent out of the chair. Grandma Trilby looks towards the window at her make-believe audience.

"Stand up, lady!" Her voice booms baritone.

"Stand up!" I say in our make-believe opera.

"You don't want to pee in your pants!" Grandma finishes the phrase, motionless in her chair. "Oh, everything is . . ."

"Work?" I offer.

"Everything is difficult. Standing up. Sitting down. Going to bed. Now getting up." She takes a breath, then exhales. "I can't get up."

I lean in and wrap my arms around her in a bear hug. I lift her, careful not to pull or push on anything. I become an extension of her body.

"I know how. Just take my word for it," I say.

"I know you know how," she says, sounding annoyed. Grandma resists at first, then rises.

"Okay, run for it." Grandma hobbles in the direction my hands lead her. At first, her wide gait looks stiff. Her body rocks side to side as if she were a cardboard cut-out of herself.

Chapter 5: People

"Step," I announce, and she lifts a foot over the metal lip separating the living room carpet from the kitchen tile.

Grandma was born Esther Levitsky. Soon after birth, she was diagnosed with severe rickets. Her mother, Bubbe Razel, placed Esther waist-high in cow manure and left her there for three days. She was cured. Six years later, Esther and her four siblings, her mother, father, and two uncles boarded a ship in Russia and sailed to New York. They all lived in a one-bedroom tenement—a common sight on Hopkinson Avenue in 1912.

"Step," I say again to Grandma at the lip of the bathroom tile.

After eleven years in Brooklyn as Esther, Grandma chose her name, Trilby, from Svengali. Grandma had played a part in a grade-school play. Trilby—the diva entranced by the evil hypnotist—could find a job. Trilby wasn't a Jewish name.

"Good luck," I say and place Grandma's hand on the bathroom sink.

Trilby studied modern dance under dance pioneers Martha Graham and Doris Humphrey.

Grandma steadies herself. I step back. I feel like a creepy voyeur. I make sure she pulls her pants down, and then I walk out. I track her progress in the bathroom from the kitchen. I stare out the window above the sink. The sun has set, and the lights that line the city below warp through the old windowpanes. I love San Francisco for the hills, for the fog that rolls in unannounced, for the constant hide-and-seek of the coast below.

Grandpa Elfryn built Grandma's rickety wooden house at the top of a hill in Diamond Heights. He died fifty-one years ago. Grandma Trilby has lived in the house without Grandpa Elfryn for more years than she had lived with him. The one-bedroom house stands out on the block. Once surrounded by eucalyptus trees and farmland, it now sits awkwardly between three-storey mansions and perfectly manicured lawns.

I walk back into the bathroom. Grandma rests with her eyes closed and rubs a spot on her scalp with her right hand. I grab a tin of shea butter from the shelf. I nail a chunk out and smear it on my palm. I warm it up in quick circular motions. It turns from paste to oil. I dab it on the scabs lining the side of her scalp.

"You know, I'll tell you, Rachel, there's a lot that happens in life that you can't put your finger on it now." Grandma knocks the dentures out of her mouth with her tongue and hands them to me. I rinse them under the running tap. "But just get much older, you can be younger than I am, and they suddenly appear. Things like, my brother used to play the violin—this was the First World War—and he would play for the soldiers who were maimed."

I wrap toilet paper around the four fingers on my left hand. "My brother took me for years. I must have blocked it out of my mind, and now I know why."

I hand Grandma the wad of toilet paper and begin rolling a new one.

"Do you know all they had was their torsos? And they put them in bird cages, and they were hanging all around the walls of the warehouse on meat hooks."

"In cages?" I respond. I wrap my arms around her and lift her from the toilet seat. She keeps her legs spread apart and begins to wipe.

"That was the First World War! All they had was here-to-here; no arms, no legs. And it affected me so . . . that I wiped it out of my memory."

Chapter 5: People

I slip the second wad of toilet paper off my fingers. I peer into the toilet bowl—dark, hard pebbles. Not bad, I think. At least there's something. I wipe Grandma's butt and drop the wad into the toilet. She flushes.

"And it came back now, it all comes back now, everything that's happened."

"Why do you think it comes back?" I ask. "Because you try so hard to forget it."

I hand Grandma her toothbrush. She still has four teeth, two on top and two on the bottom.

"I wish I could have met some of your friends," I say through a mouth full of white suds. I decided to brush my teeth, too. My words come out garbled.

Grandma spits into the sink.

"Well, when I was young, you know, still in public school, I had Bella Puro and Gertrude Ruben. They were my best friends, the two of them. Gertrude Ruben and Bella Puro. And Florence Lipschitz! The three. This was in Brooklyn."

Grandma dries each finger methodically.

"The Lipschitz' were the aristocrats. And she befriended me? I stuck my chest out!"

Grandma shuts her eyes and shuffles slowly toward her bedroom, gliding her hands along the wall. She reaches out for the top of the radiator to navigate through the doorframe. Grandma keeps her eyes closed.

I walk into the bedroom before her and stand beside the remote-controlled single bed. I pull the top sheet down, and the blankets fold with it. I rearrange the three pillows. Grandma sits on the edge of the bed. I bend to help her raise her left calf. We swing together, aiming for the centre of the bed. I hand Grandma her Codewords book and a pen.

Chocolate hides above the refrigerator. If she eats too much, Grandma's scalp itches unbearably. She knows this, but still, it's a fight. I unwrap a bar as quietly as I can and pop three squares into my mouth. I find the phone under a dishtowel and dial home.

"Hello?" Dad picks up.

"Hey, it's me. Is it too late?" Toronto is three hours ahead.

"No, we're just lying here. How's it going out there?"

"Good, but Grandma only had a tiny shit today. Rabbit poo."

"Put the cilium in her morning shake."

I open the pantry door. "What does it look like?"

Dad and I talk for a while, but I could tell he was sleeping when I called. He agrees to pick me up at the airport on Sunday. I imagine being back in my apartment: laundry, midterms, work at the bar, and a lover I barely like. My bike is broken, and the fridge will be empty.

I find Grandma asleep, chin to chest. I lean in and press my cheek softly against hers. She stiffens for a moment, then sighs, knowing it is me, without opening her eyes. Her flesh is more forgiving than mine.

"Come in," she growls. "There's room."

"Okay."

She hacks into a tissue she pulls from her sleeve. I take the tissue and toss it into the wastebasket beside her bed.

"Let's watch something," she says.

Grandma can barely make out the images on the TV screen. I take the wireless earphones off the bedside table and click the power switch. I hand them to Grandma. She bends them open and inches them into her ears like a stethoscope.

Chapter 5: People

"Is it a talkie?" she asks.

"Silent. But it's Greta Garbo—and she's young!"

"Oh, my."

Grandma listens to the lonely call of a single violin crescendo. Garbo twirls frantically around a mob of masked characters. A clarinet sounds through the chaos, depicting the carnivalesque masquerade.

"She sees a man," I yell, pulling out her left earphone. "They take their masks off! She's enchanted with him!"

"Oh, right." Grandma laughs. "I think I know this one."

～

"Hello?" I know Grandma answers her phone in the living room. She never picks up when she's in her bedroom.

"Grandma, it's Rachel." I strain to be both loud and relaxed. "How are you?"

"Oh, Rachel. I'm the last rose of summer."

"I've been writing down the stories you told me when I visited last," I say.

She laughs. "Well, everything changes, my dear, in one's mind."

"How do you mean?"

"Each day is not the same when you get to my age. What happened then and what you think now, each day it's different."

Chapter 6: Places

Write about a place. Present details of incidents, people, setting and landscape to show the place. Show a place by showing what happens in it.

The Back Stairwell

Saamiyah Ali-Mohammed

> *The whole earth is a masjid (place for prayer) and pure*
> *... the Prophet Muhammad said.*

Frigid winter wind seeps in through the doorway and ruffles my purple crepe headscarf. Icy mist frosts the floor-to-ceiling window. I pray for the first time in the back stairwell of the Davis Building at the University of Toronto Mississauga.

A fleece glove lies abandoned on the windowsill. A fly smacks into the window and buzzes down the glass. My toes curl on the cement. Professor Khan's voice squawks over a microphone in the adjoining lecture hall. He answers students' questions during the ten-minute break, too short a break to walk all the way to the prayer room.

A door opens and voices echo in the stairwell above me. The door whooshes shut. Boots clunk on the stairs. The door that leads into the lecture hall thuds open against the concrete wall.

"Bipolar involves both depressive and manic episodes," Professor Khan says. "On the other hand, depression—"

The door swings closed and muffles Professor Khan's voice.

I stand in qiyām. I learned at age three to fold my right hand over my left hand and then place them both on my chest. I learned to fix my eyes on the floor and memorized verses from the Qu'rān.

Qiyām: Standing for the recitation of al-Fātiḥah and other verses of the Qu'rān.

Chapter 6: Places

I look down, rest my hands on my chest and whisper verses into the silence.

37. [Abraham said] "O our Lord! I have made some of my offspring to dwell in an uncultivable valley by Your Sacred House (Ka' bah), so that they may perform prayer . . .

40. "O my Lord, make me and my offspring among those who perform prayer. And accept my invocation."

I bow down in rukū' and splay my fingers over my knees. I keep my back straight while I bow and after I rise.

 Rukū': Bowing at the waist.

I crouch in sujūd and the grain of the concrete floor digs into my forehead. In Arabic, sujūd means "to submit." In prayer, sujūd refers to prostration and the placement of seven body parts on the floor: the forehead (including the nose), both hands, both knees and the bottoms of the toes of both feet. Sujūd symbolizes complete submission to God in all aspects of life.

 *Sujūd: Prostration*

I sit up and then prostrate again. The Prophet Muhammad sometimes recited verses aloud in qiyām. His companions, tribal leaders and jinns (spiritual beings) stopped to listen.

When in sujūd, he only whispered.

The Back Stairwell

The wind whistles. A toilet flushes in the women's washroom across the hall. My eyelids droop. I mouth the words.

The door at the top of the staircase swings open and rattles against the wall. Dust puffs up like talcum powder. A guy and a girl walk down the stairs. Coffee sloshes onto the steps. The guy giggles, steps onto the landing and stops mid-giggle.

My heart beats faster. The floor bites into my knees. I hiss my praise of God.

I jump up, crack my knuckles and murmur under my breath. My lips fumble and I mispronounce all the Arabic words.

1. Say: He is Allah, the one and only
2. Allah, the eternal, absolute
3. He begetteth not nor is He begotten.
4. And there is none like unto Him.

I stare at the replica of the Ka'bah (Muslim house of worship in Mecca) woven into the top of my dark blue sajjadah, a prayer mat that Muslims orient to face the Ka'bah before we begin prayer. My sneakers sit at its edge.

I rock on the balls of my bare feet.

The girl's heeled boots click and the boy's sneakers squelch in a musical beat as they pass. "Come on," she says. The door behind me creaks open and bangs closed. The clicks fade as they walk down the hallway.

I bow down, straighten, and fall into sujūd. My glasses clack against the concrete. I sit back on my heels, praise the Prophet, then mutter, "Assalamu alaikum (Peace be upon you)." The angels greeted the first man and prophet, Prophet Adam, with these words. Muslims greet each other with these words. We also say assalamu

Chapter 6: Places

alaikum to the angels, and to the worshippers left and right of us to signify the end of the prayer.

A blonde hair clings to the hem of my sajjadah. I brush off the hair, fold my sajjadah into a rectangle and tuck it into my coat pocket. I yank on my running shoes, run up the stairs and duck into class.

"Where were you?" asks Amanjit as I slide back into the seat next to her.

"I bought a coffee," I say.

Amanjit frowns. "I was there."

"I was . . . I was praying, actually," I say.

"Oh," she says. "You could have just said so."

Finding the Moon

Jonathan Waugh

Caleigh looked up at me grimly. "How long to the top?" she asked. Sweat dripped down the side of her face.

"Uhhhhh, I think we're about halfway." I guessed. The sun was high in the California sky. The sweat beaded on my forehead and stung as it dripped into my eyes.

Caleigh squinted. "It doesn't look like halfway," she mused. Her brow furrowed and unfurrowed.

"I know. I think distance can be deceiving in the mountains, though. Stuff can look further than it is."

I hoped I was right.

We carried on after a water break, eager to get to the top. The sun was high in the sky, there was no wind, and we saw few other hikers. The top of Freel Peak was just under eleven thousand feet, and we could see it in the distance. We talked about our trip to that point—this was the last big hike we would do before we continued to San Francisco and then finally to Austin, Texas. California made me feel an odd nostalgia, though I had only visited a couple of times. It was my first time sharing that experience with Caleigh.

We had spent almost two weeks in the backcountry before this, in Yosemite, in Tuolumne meadows, in Lone Pine, and finally in a campsite in South Lake Tahoe. Caleigh had never backpacked before, but we cruised through the high Sierras without any issues. We had decided to climb this mountain the night before while we lay in our tent and looked at the stars.

Chapter 6: Places

～

The sun beat down on us, and our breathing became more laboured as we left the cool confines of the conifer forests and clambered into the barren high alpine rock and snow. Small tufts of grass swayed in the breeze.

"I have a headache," Caleigh said.

"Do you want to stop?" I asked.

Caleigh was quiet as we continued. "We're a lot closer now, right?"

I looked up. We were much closer, the peak coming into view as the snow got thicker around us.

"Yeah, we're closer now, I think. Maybe forty-five minutes from the top."

"Okay, let's keep going then. If we stop, I don't think I'll be able to get back up."

We ambled over the summer snowpack, the white snow streaked with black dirt and spotted with red, alpine algae. The hard granules slipped over the tops of our boots and soaked our socks. We were so close, though. We stopped again for water, and I looked at my GPS. We had gone sixteen kilometers so far and had gained five thousand feet of elevation from the parking lot. Caleigh looked haggard, and I felt haggard.

"Do you feel okay?" I asked.

"No." She wiped her mouth. "Let's keep going."

The last five hundred metres to the summit were a sprint. We didn't talk until we crested over bare rock, and there was nothing in front of us except the state of Nevada—eight thousand feet below. I laughed, Caleigh cried, and we hugged and high-fived in a dizzy celebration. The sun sat lower in the western sky than when we started, and we realized we still had seventeen kilometres to go before we got back to the parking lot.

"At least it's downhill," Caleigh said. We marched down, back through our path in the snow.

"My legs are so sore," I said. I rubbed my thighs as I walked.

"Same. We're not going to be able to walk tomorrow."

The sun was behind the mountain when we got back to the safety of the pine forests.

Caleigh and I shared her apple. I ate all of my snacks at the summit. We looked forward to sitting.

"Okay, now we're actually close," I said. "Remember this gnarled tree I pointed out when we started?"

Caleigh snorted. "Sure."

I smiled.

We returned to the car an hour later, and the sun had fully set. We winded down the small road, laughing about my concept of "close," and talking about the small marmot we had seen. The sky was a light violet, and as we turned around a steep bend to face east, we saw the full moon perched above the Freel Peak. We were silent.

"That's so pretty," Caleigh said.

"I know. It looks so big when it's on the horizon." I looked at Caleigh and smiled. "I'm proud of you for finishing that hike. We could have turned around at any point, but you wanted to keep going."

"I know. Once we got up there, I had to finish it." She gestured to the moon rising over the mountain. "It's kind of like the mountain is thanking us for climbing it."

One Morning in Singapore

Gabrielle Ong

Eighty percent of Singaporeans live in public Housing Development Board apartments, affectionately called HDB. Ninety percent of residents own their flat. They call it home.

My home is on the sixth floor of a twelve-storey block. An identical block opposite us mirrors our grid of flats, as though I am the middle piece of a Jenga Tower. Here, I have the perfect view.

The *void deck* is the first level of the block: a common space. Uncles and aunties sit at the stone seats to chat and play chess, children ride their bicycles and play soccer, and residents hold weddings, funerals, and birthday parties.

Above the void deck, an open corridor runs across each storey, connecting the flats. Neighbours bump into one another to get to their homes. Some stop to chat, and others hurry past. The father of Unit #04-898 always lingers at his front door and stares at his phone before he finally steps in.

Unit #06-894 likes to keep their windows and doors wide open. I gaze into their house, past their furniture, past moving shadows, through the windows, to the sky on the other side.

Every year during National Day, each house hangs the national flag on their part of the corridor. The red and white flags appear one by one, like pieces of a tic-tac-toe grid, forming lines, clusters and patterns. Unit #12-880 is not patriotic and never hangs a flag. It leaves a hole in the otherwise perfect grid.

When I study, I peek over at Unit #08-896. Sometimes, a girl my age sits at her desk and faces the window with her head down. Occasionally, our eyes meet. She grins with embarrassment, and her shoulders heave. I do the same. We flash a thumbs-up at each other and glance down at our books.

~~

The clock reads 6:47 am. It is still dark. The shrill, sharp crows of someone's stupid rooster awakens me.

"Gabby, 7:02 am, don't be late for your school bus!" Dad hollers from the kitchen. The microwave hums. Two minutes and thirty seconds for me to wash up.

I stare at my reflection in the bathroom mirror and tie my hair into a neat ponytail. I button up my white blouse, throw on my navy-blue pinafore, and buckle the matching belt. The pleats of my pinafore are wrinkled, even though I ironed them yesterday. Their folds press against my skin. I tug at the creases and straighten them out.

I rush to the kitchen, gulp down my daily breakfast of runny, microwaved eggs and two vitamins, and rush to the door. Dad waits for me, ready to run down the corridor and press the elevator button. I tie my shoelaces, run after him, and step into the waiting elevator.

It takes thirteen seconds for the elevator to descend and one extra second before the doors open.

The smell of fresh blood pierces my nose.

Next to the playground, cops stand at the grass patch. Their navy-blue uniforms blend into the darkness of dawn, except for the white gloves that glisten on their hands.

Chapter 6: Places

"Block 8223 Sims Road, uhm . . . we've got a male jumper," one stammers into his radio.

The cops form a circle and spread a black sheet over the jumper. Within the circle, below the sheet, lie large chunks. One chunk, covered in clothes, looks like a ball.

The black sheet lowers.

One cop stands further away from the rest. He approaches a stump in the grass. He hesitates, bends down, then picks it up. The end of the stump has five bloody fingers.

"Gabby, go go! Your bus is waiting!" Dad plants his hands on my shoulders and swings me away. The bus honks twice. I sprint towards it, stand at the door, turn around, wave to my dad, and climb up the steps.

The bus is dark inside. Everyone usually naps during the precious drive to school. My heart thumps, my shoulders tremble, and my gaze averts from the sleeping bodies beside me.

How long did he stand in the corridor?
Didn't anybody see or hear him?
Didn't anybody give him a thumbs-up?

We turn into the last road before reaching school. Sunlight floods the bus. My bus mates stir and rub their eyes.

I pretend to do the same.

Three days later, a funeral appears on the void deck.

My parents never say a word about the incident. In Asian culture, it is bad to talk about death. Chanting monks and resonating gongs of the funeral disturb my studies. I stay late in school to study until the three-day funeral ends.

A year passes. The week around that September day, at that spot of grass, mourners plant burning joss sticks into the soil and stack preservative-filled oranges on a paper plate: a peace offering to the gods. The smell of incense rises six storeys to my room where I study.

Deep in Southern Alberta

Helen Sproule

Sweat gathers from my pores and drips down my back. The sun strikes the dry crunchy grass and hard earth beneath me. John, a friend of my father's, and I, sixteen, stand on a hill somewhere deep in Southern Alberta.

John, the only person in southern Canada with a permit to track and band endangered birds of prey, got me on the permit this year. I helped him with the banding for the past two years. John now wants to train me, so I can take over for him one day.

I glance back at John, a short distance behind me. John names the plants we pass. I interject with mmhmms. He wears light blue jeans patched up with brown canvas, an off-white thick long-sleeve button-up shirt, a pair of hiking boots he has owned for twenty years, and a dark brown leather safari hat. His perfectly trimmed moustache stands out.

I reach the end of the steep portion of the hill. I turn around and scan the landscape of valleys and hills and cliffs and the small gravel road that curves through the middle. I lift my Nikon I320, flick it on, and peer through the viewfinder. I press the shutter release and rotate the lens clockwise as far as it goes. The camera zooms in on John's distant truck: a rusted light blue 1988 Ford F-150. We walk alone out here.

The insects buzz, the crickets chirp, and John says, "I really think you'll look back and regret it if you don't record amazing experiences like these." John has encouraged me to record my summer experiences in a journal since the start of summer.

I turn to John, wrinkle my nose and smile. He knows from my smile that I haven't started. John continues, "You'll forget everything if you don't write it down. You're so lucky. This is not something anyone else gets to do."

We march along. I remove my safari hat and fan myself. We are close to a nest. We hear the shrieking of a pair of prairie falcons, a mother and a father, who have left their nest to circle above us.

―――

John's father, the first person to breed peregrine falcons in captivity, became a famous, falconer. John's father toured hundreds of sites in Southern Alberta to band raptors. He did this for the government. John accompanied his father to the sites and took over when his father got too old.

Each band has a number. The numbers refer to a log with species, site location, gender, and age of the chicks. That way, we can track the population's movement, growth, decline, and reasons for deaths.

John met my father in Denmark where they both worked after university. They became close friends through their interest in birds. My dad grew up with two pet ducks and later, once he had his own house, he bred finches, tanagers, and canaries for the Aviculture Society's repopulation project. When he moved with my mother and two older sisters from Oakville to Calgary years later, he and John reconnected.

―――

Chapter 6: Places

An old fence post stands at the top of a drop. We swing around the post to the other side. I step up and climb along the cliff to the nest. Prairie falcons' nest in tiny caves in cliffs to protect their young from predators.

"How many are there?" John shouts. He climbs to join me.

I glance beside me. Eight eyes stare at me. "Four." One of the chicks presses against my thigh. Somehow, this chick feels warm, even in the dry heat.

"Are they old enough to band?"

"No, they look about two weeks old." They sit with their mouths open and glare at me with wide black eyes. These tiny white fluffballs the size of my fist try to appear threatening. I pick one up and hold it out for John to see. He reaches the ledge and perches on the other end of the groove.

He chuckles. "Give me your camera. I want to take a picture of you with those bright red nails holding a falcon." The first time John took me banding I had my nails painted pink. That amused John so I always paint them every time we go. I place the chick in my lap and hand John my camera. I don't like to be photographed, but I usually let John take a couple. He struggles to turn on the camera, then takes a couple of photos. He ensures he snapped my bright red manicure in the photos.

We have to band the birds at three weeks old. Any younger and they are too small for the bands. Any older and they get grabby with their razor-sharp talons, a lesson I carry in the marks on my forearms.

The mother dives at us. I take my camera back from John and wait for her to dive again. She swoops down at us.

I get the shot.

John inspects the photos he took. We scale our way back out. My hands sweat and slip. I rush back to flat ground.

We hike over, across, and down the hill, back to the truck, and on to the next site.

Harmonica

Gauri Menon

My laptop flashes 5:00 p.m. The sun vanishes below the windowsill of Alex's living room in Roy Ivor Hall at the University of Toronto, Mississauga. Alex and I crouch in identical hard chairs and browse our Instagram feeds.

"How much longer, Anh?" Alex yells to Anh, his roommate.

"Gimme a minute!" Anh's faint voice yells from down the hallway.

I stare at my phone. My friendship with Alex started five days ago. Our mothers work at a Dubai-based marketing firm. I remember Alex's mom vaguely from corporate dinner parties. I don't even know her name.

Anh glides into the room. "Okay, let's go." A short Vietnamese Canadian, she wears a perpetual frown in her eyebrows. Alex introduced us at Frosh Week yesterday. Today she celebrates her 19th birthday.

Alex stands up, brushes cereal crumbs from his hoodie, and pockets his phone. Alex and Anh move toward the door. Alex stops and asks me for the second time that day, "Are you sure you don't want to come for our little birthday bash?"

"Fine, I'll come," I blurt. My laptop snaps shut and I trail them out the door.

We stand on the pitch-dark third floor of a quiet industrial complex. The only source of light is the store sign.

Harmonica

VAPE HUT. The wonky, blood-red letters flash a warning in my face. Beneath the letters, a plain black font announces: Only 19-Year-Olds Allowed.

I don't know the name of the building. I don't know the name of the street. I only know it took a ten-minute Uber ride that sped us over an unlit bridge to get here.

Alex and Anh march through the automatic doors. I hesitate to step over the threshold. I have never been in a vape shop before. Alex pauses and swivels to face me.

"What's the matter?" he asks. He approaches me and peers into my eyes for a minute. "Wait . . . is it hitting you?" A smug grin snakes onto his face.

"What?" I blink at him. Then, I remember how I had gulped the first edible of my life in his living room several hours earlier. It was Alex's face that goaded me to take it. "No, it's not," I state.

"I think it's hitting you."

"*No*, it's not."

The spiffy shop sparkles under fluorescent tube lights. Giant glass showcases line the wall. Each showcase has shelves and each shelf has boxes and each box holds a velvet cushion. Colourful metal cuboids rest on the cushions. The glint of shop light on metal and velvet makes the set-ups feel luxurious. They look like cases of expensive perfumes or Cartier pens or luxury creams or wedding jewellery. They look like everything in the world except vape pens.

A heavyset woman frowns at us from behind the glass counter. We approach her. A plastic nametag on her brown shirt says, LAURA.

Anh is about to speak when Laura spins to me. "What flavour do you want?" she snaps.

Chapter 6: Places

"Oh, actually . . . I'm not . . . ," I stutter.

Ahn interrupts me, "Give me Grape, please."

"Are you all nineteen?" Laura asks. I glance over at Alex who keeps quiet.

Anh wordlessly flashes her government ID. Laura glances at it in the stark light and nods. She turns to me. I shake my head.

"You're going to have to wait outside," Laura sighs. I nod and turn promptly in the direction of the door.

"But can't we just stand here? We won't do anything, geez," Alex huffs.

"Sorry. Rules are rules," Laura says with a clipped tone.

"Don't be such a—"

"We're leaving, thank you!" I interrupt Alex, grab his coat sleeve, and pull him with me.

Behind us, Laura mutters not too quietly, "Blasted kids."

"Let's go," I hiss at him. "What if she calls the police on us?"

Alex pauses, looks at me and grins. "Cops? Shit, you're definitely high, dude."

No, I'm freaking not, you freaking moron. I mouth the words.

Outside, we flap our coats to build some heat in the chill September frost. In a few minutes, Anh joins us. We stand under the broken shop awning to avoid the frozen raindrops. Anh whips out the vape pen.

"Shit, it's been so long since I had a hit," Alex says. He blows loudly into his bare hands.

Anh slips off the navy-blue cover of the purple pen. She flips open the steel lid and touches it to her mouth. She sucks air into her cheeks and puffs like a professional wind player. Now that I think about it, the vape pen does resemble a high-end harmonica.

I watch Anh and Alex take huge swigs. The bottom of the pen lights up with each puff. The electric letters of VAPE HUT above us begin to short-circuit and die.

The sign now reads V PE HUT. Alex extends the pen to me. I stare at it without moving.

"Oh! Of course, *you* don't want a hit, do you, your High . . . ness?" Alex's maniacal giggle sends embarrassed shockwaves down my spine.

V PE HUT becomes V E HUT. The scent of spicy mint and rotten grapes hangs in the billows of smoke around me. I try not to breathe it in. Anh digs her cold hands into my right coat pocket. I let her.

This is definitely what my mom wanted for me when she introduced me to Alex, I think.

V E HUT becomes V H T. Alex and Ahn puff away in the glow of the three letters. When the sign sputters out completely, we book an Uber home.

Two weeks later, I click the small Instagram notification that lights my phone. The screen refreshes and lands on a new post by Alex_Viper. Alex holds out gang signs at an unknown intersection in the evening. His black hoodie covers most of the frame. A burning cigarette butt in his mouth, the only source of light, throws long shadows across his face. I read the caption.

VAPES ARE FOR WIMPS. SMOKE LIKE A VIPER.

I continue to scroll through my Instagram feed.

The fall term came and went, and then the winter and then the summer. I never saw Alex or Anh again.

The Elevator

Bayan Khatib

Even with the darkness of the night and the gentle rocking of the van as my uncle drives, even with my head on Nana's warm lap, I can't fall asleep.

"Only a few more minutes," my uncle calls out.

In only a few minutes I will meet my parents for the first time since I was a baby. I have lived with my grandparents for the past seven years. It has taken Grandfather seven years to find a way to reunite me with my parents in America.

A few weeks ago Nana, the only mother I have known, told me that she is not my mother—she's my grandmother.

"This is your mother, your father, your brother and your sisters," she said as she showed me pictures. "Your mother is very nice and she's going to take very good care of you."

It felt like Nana was telling me an imaginary story.

My grandparents and I flew to Mississippi, where my eldest uncle lives. As soon as my uncle got a break from work, we started driving to Denver, Colorado, where my real family lives.

After hours and hours of driving, my uncle finally says, "We're here." He parks the van in front of an old brown building. A man and a woman run down the stairs from an upstairs apartment.

"That's them," my uncle says.

Someone lifts me off the ground into a tight embrace. I feel kisses all over my face. Tears stream down the cheeks of the woman who holds me so tightly. The man beside her takes me from her and hugs me and kisses me and carries me up the stairs into a small apartment.

"The kids fell asleep," my mother says, as if she were apologizing. "They tried hard to stay awake, but it got too late. They were really excited to meet their new sister."

"I'll go wake them up," my father says.

"They can wait till tomorrow."

But my father is already in the bedroom. Seconds later, three wide-awake children, ages three, four and five, walk out and sit next to my mother on the floor. My father introduces us to each other. None of us say anything. We stare at each other as the adults speak.

I sleep on the floor and Nana cuddles me as she does every night. I will soon have to learn how to sleep without Nana's arms around me.

In the beginning, my brother wants to give me all his toys. In the beginning, I think being a big sister might be fun.

After a few weeks, everything changes.

One morning, my brother tells me that he wants to show me something in the building across the street. I love adventure. My brother and I run to the building. We walk through the dim, empty entrance.

"Do you know what that is?" my brother asks.

"No."

"It's an elevator."

"What's an elevator?"

"Come, I'll show you."

My brother presses the "UP" button. The elevator door opens, and we walk in together. He presses 20, the highest number on the

Chapter 6: Places

side panel. Just before the door closes completely, my brother runs out of the elevator. I stand alone. The door shuts, and the elevator starts to move. I push and hit the door. It won't open. I watch the numbers light up on the panel—3, 4, 5, 6, 7—until it finally reaches 20.

The door opens and I run out. I look around. I see nothing. I hear nothing. I feel scared. I sit on the floor in front of the elevator and cry and cry and cry. I think about Nana and cry. I think about my home in Syria and cry. I think about my new family and cry.

A woman with two children walks to the elevator and presses the "DOWN" button. She looks at me. I look at her. She asks me questions that I don't understand.

"I don't speak English," I say in Arabic.

"You speak Arabic?"

"Yes."

"Why are you crying?"

"I don't know how to go back home."

"Where do you live?"

"I don't know."

"What's your mother's name?"

I don't know what to answer. I want to tell her Nana's name, but I know she wouldn't know Nana. She might know Mama.

"Do you know a woman named Dawn?"

"Yes," the woman replies. "She's my friend. She lives in the building across from here. Oh my God, are you Dawn's daughter, the one who just came from Syria?"

"Yes."

"Come with me. I'll take you to her."

The Elevator

Nana taught me to never go anywhere with a stranger, but this woman seems my only hope of ever getting back to Nana. I follow the lady back to my parents' apartment. My mother hugs me as she thanks her friend over and over.

I tell my mother what my brother did to me. He runs to his room. Mama runs after him and shuts my brother's door behind her. I hear her yell. I hear him scream. I feel nothing for him.

～

The next morning, my father takes me back to the building and teaches me how to use an elevator.

Door FiftyFive

Miguel DaSilva

Raymond, our head chef at the whiskey bar Door FiftyFive, drops a parachute onto my workstation. The parachute, a tiny scrunched-up piece of rolling paper no bigger than a Smartie, contains a hit of molly.

"Take this when you want," Raymond says. "Do you think you can do your close in an hour?"

"Yeah man, fuck it, we should just roll right now," I say. I pocket the parachute and wipe down my stainless-steel workstation.

"You're wild. Are you sure you can finish the close high?"

"Heck yeah, I'll take it in thirty minutes, I'll almost be done, it'll hit me when I have ten minutes left, and I'll be rolling by the time Deejay pours our 3 Speed."

"Okay." Raymond laughs, a canine juts from his smile.

Raymond walks to the expo station (the expo loads food on trays for delivery to the diners) and cleans. Raymond wears a tank top these nights after the ovens are turned off, but the air still holds heat. His tribal tattoos with elk and deer and owls trail around his thick forearms. He went to college for a couple of years after high school, but school wasn't his thing, so he dropped out and became a bodybuilder, with broad round shoulders and sharp triceps, a bulked-up chest, and a tiny spiky-haired head. He works quickly, methodically, professionally. Raymond squeezes orange sanitizer onto each surface, each leg, each edge, each shelf and dries them all with a clean rag.

Door FiftyFive

He finishes the expo station, scrubs down the grill, scrapes gunk off the Salamander oven, and changes the foil and the wood chips in the smoker. I clean the tall stainless-steel table and the small fridge behind me, stocked with chicken wings, sauces, mozzarella sticks, burgers, pickles, fries, all the food Raymond prepped this morning before I came in.

Door FiftyFive, a small whiskey bar on Queen Street in Streetsville, remains quiet most nights. On Fridays and Saturdays, four-dollar shots of Jack Daniel's turn the bar into a writhing mess, and a live DJ plays a pop playlist to awkward grinding and shuffling.

Wooden beams cross the length of the ceiling. Logs stacked like bricks cover the walls. A life-sized Captain Morgan statue, that silly pirate with a pointy goatee and a foot raised over a barrel of rum, stands next to the entrance. A glowing blue ATM sits next to Captain Morgan. Tables run along an open-concept floor, the bar glows with dim neon green and blue lights. Bolted-down cocktail tables stretch across the middle of the floor, and large windows peek out onto the side patio and the construction site across the lot. Two mute televisions, perpetually on *SportsCentre*, hang behind the bar and a glass mirror behind them reflects liquor bottle labels.

The kitchen looks bright, chrome-plated, sterile and clean, with blank green walls and white tiles. The hood fan's yawning drone whirs, and a rich oak smell wafts in plumes above the smoker.

It feels too bright, especially when I'm high.

Raymond turns to me around midnight and says he finished. I'm only halfway done, so we pull out our parachutes, touch them in a cheer, and swallow the Zig-Zag paper filled with MDMA. We always shake our heads at each other when we do that. We raise our eyebrows and shrug.

Chapter 6: Places

Raymond helps me close since I'm pretty much useless on molly. I sigh every twenty-five seconds. Sigh and stretch, rub my eyes with clenched fists, open and close my mouth, flex my jaw, lick my lips. I do everything but check labels for expiry dates, filter the fryer oil, or sweep behind the appliances.

"Are you peaking already?" Raymond eyes me with a little smile, arms soaked to the elbows in dirty water at the sink.

"No, man, I'm fine," I say. I swing the mop bucket around and a wave of dirty water cascades onto the oven and across the floor Raymond swept. I walk to one of the counters and rest my elbows on the cold stainless steel. Sweat collects against my forehead and drips over my eyebrows and rolls off my cheek and splashes onto the counter. I wipe it away with my forearm and more sweat erupts from my face. Am I peaking? It's been, I check the clock on the wall, an hour. Shit.

"Aha, you *are* peaking. I'll finish this. Go get changed."

I grab the walls all the way to the employee area. I change, stare at myself in the washroom mirror, and rub my elbows, my shoulders, my chest.

The yellow bulb, dull most days, drowns my vision in blinding light.

Raymond barges in with bulging eyes and a fishy smile. "So, you're fucked, eh?"

"Oh yeah."

"Awesome. Also, close your eyes a bit," he squeaks.

"You close your eyes a bit, buddy. Don't talk shit," I say with my finger next to his eye.

"Reach the bar, we're going to Adrienne's. Hawk is here, and we're gonna get even more fucked up."

Door FiftyFive

I follow him upstairs and almost moan. The air caresses my skin. I pull out a stool, sit next to Hawk, and ask Deejay why the lights are so bright.

"They're no different today, asshole. You're high," Deejay says. He removes his beanie and rubs his massive hands against his bald head. He's the bartender, but he could be the bouncer like all the other 'roided out juice heads Door FiftyFive hires.

"No, we are not, Mr. Deejay. Mind your own business anyway," Raymond says.

"Okay, so I guess I'll mind my business when you want a free pint." He pulls the tall frosty glass of 3 Speed away from the counter.

Raymond raises one finger. "Wait, no, no, no. I take that back. I'm sorry, Deejay, please give me free pints."

We all laugh, and I moan. We laugh again while Raymond and Deejay mock me with ridiculous porno grunts and heaves. Deejay picks up a bottle of vodka from the rail and turns to serve one of the old men that sit in silence and drink alone. Hawk and Raymond look at me. "You're actually high, though, aren't you?" Raymond teases.

"Umm, Raymond, can you tell me just what in the rolling hell you gave me?" I ask.

Raymond's hand, covered in small burns and tiny scars, wipes away his sweat and the sweat from my forehead. Then, he hugs me. "I love ya, buddy." He exhales and sighs.

"Oh fuck, that feels amazing, buddy," I say. Human touch feels like a feather tickling my skin.

We down extra shots of Jack, pay for them and jump into Raymond's black Hyundai Veloster. Deep house music punctuates

Chapter 6: Places

the potholes and sewer covers. I stare out the window. My head vibrates against the glass, and I picture myself diving into a clear blue grotto. I shiver. The greens and yellows and reds from the traffic lights streak across my blurred vision and my pupils dance in my sockets and the world vibrates and I close my eyes and run my fingertips across the tiny brown hairs on my arm, across my chest, around my neck and tug at the beard on my chin while my head lolls. My dry lips curl into a painful smile and I draw in a shallow breath.

Chapter 7: Work

*Write about a job you have held or observed.
Choose one incident, a series of incidents, or a
period of time to demonstrate features of the job.*

Code Blue

Mia Ortega

"Code blue, ER. Code blue, ER." The voice on the intercom jars me from my book, *Harry Potter and the Chamber of Secrets*. The printer whines behind me, filling Care Regional Medical Centre's small x-ray reception office with its mechanical whir. I remove my feet from the desk, set the book down, yawn, stretch my arms, and glance at the bright blue computer screen. December 28, 2016, 3:15 a.m. I stand up, clip my dosimeter and badge back on, smooth down my grey scrubs, and grab the warm sheet of paper.

John Doe, 1-year-old, 1 view chest x-ray, portable. My eyebrows draw together. A code blue, at three in the morning, on an infant. A code blue call requires all available staff to aid the person who needs cardiac or respiratory resuscitation. John Doe means the information hasn't been verified fast enough for the order to be written, and the one-view chest x-ray is standard for any code blue call.

I fold the sheet of paper and stuff it into my scrub pocket. I zip out of the office and cross the hall, passing by the mammography, ultrasound, and x-ray rooms. Cold air and the aroma of disinfectant breeze past my face as I scurry to grab an imaging plate from its storage place. I retrace my steps back to the hallway and pry open the storage compartment of the portable x-ray machine. The imaging plate slides in with a thud, resounding with a clang. I unplug the charging cord from the wall and turn a large grey knob. The machine chirps to life with a beep, and green numbers flash on a small screen. My hands clench down on a long bar—the wheels unlock

Chapter 7: Work

and lurch forward—and I push the thousand-pound camera like a shopping cart down the winding hallways until I reach the double doors of the Emergency Room.

The ER holds four stretchers separated by curtains, two small rooms, and two trauma rooms. I edge the machine forward, careful not to hit any bystanders. The Code Blue soundtrack includes: a cacophony of voices shouting orders, medical supplies palmed and torn open, footsteps bustling, scrubs rustling, vital sign monitors whining, and someone crying. The night-shift staff buzzes in and out of Trauma Room A. I pass a couple being escorted and consoled by the triage nurse. The woman wails into the man's chest. I avert my eyes back to my machine and push into the room.

"X-ray is here," a nurse says to the doctor while she hangs an IV bag.

"Good," he says. "Stand by."

Six nurses and the doctor crowd around the stretcher in the centre of the room, creating a wall of grey scrubs. I park the x-ray machine on the side, out of the way, and stand with my back straight and hands interlaced. A nurse leaves to grab more medical supplies and I finally see John Doe.

The baby, with skin tinted grey, limbs immobile, lies silent and still on the stretcher. One nurse tilts his head back and locks an oxygen mask onto his tiny mouth. Another nurse scissors away the top and bottom of his *Toy Story* pyjamas. Another nurse on the opposite side of the stretcher begins chest compressions, pumping two fingers up and down the middle of his bare chest. They raise him to swipe the pyjamas away and onto the floor where they join the clutter of instrument wrappers.

"Patient story?" the doctor asks.

Code Blue

A nurse with a chart in her hand says, "The mother went to check on her baby in the middle of the night. He was tangled in the sheets. When she uncovered him, he wasn't moving or breathing."

One of my fingers twitches. I realize I've been holding my breath. The nurse with the IV bag shakes her head.

"I'm unable to get an IV started. Veins are too small." She chucks the needle into the red bin behind her.

"Intraosseous infusion," the doctor replies without taking his eyes off the vital signs monitor. I recall reading the procedure in a textbook: a needle is inserted straight into the bone marrow, giving direct access to infuse fluids or drugs. Two nurses race toward the glass storage cabinets, hands flying through an assortment of large white packets, adding to the litter of wrappers on the floor.

The IV nurse comes back with a small drill gun. She grips the baby's right leg with her hand and points the drill gun straight at his shin. My eyes widen. The needle connects with flesh. The high-pitched drill whirs. Metal scrapes against bone. I clench my teeth and stare at the dull grey walls. The nurse puts down the drill gun and connects the IV to its new port.

They say an intraosseous infusion is extremely painful, but there are no cries. Not a sound from the baby except for the CPR's artificial heartbeat echoing on the monitor. The baby moves only when the nurses shift his limbs or pump his chest.

"We're going to be here for a while," the doctor says to me. I nod. I leave the x-ray machine in case they call later for the chest x-ray. I walk back to the x-ray reception room and put on my jacket. It's colder than usual. I pick up my phone and look up funny cat videos on YouTube.

An hour later, the office phone rings.

Chapter 7: Work

"X-ray. This is Mia," I answer.

"Hey, Mia. You can cancel the order. It's not needed anymore."

"Okay. Thanks." I hang up. I press the home button on my iPhone and stare at the screen till it fades and finally turns to black. The only reason they would cancel is if the baby didn't make it. I get up and head back to the ER to retrieve the x-ray machine. I stuff my hands into my scrub pockets and remind myself this is normal.

Fishmonger

Halah Butt

A dusty bicycle leans on its stand on Ammi's driveway in Karachi, Pakistan. The front wheel tips sideways from the weight of the wicker basket attached to the handlebars. The machli wala, Urdu for fishmonger, sets down the rusted iron scale he had balanced across his shoulders. The scale, made of flat round dishes hanging from a pole, holds two large fish—their grey skin glints in the sunlight and their yellow eyes bulge from pink heads. Palm fronds hang over the concrete walls that surround my grandmother's property.

The sunny, August afternoon in 2014 marks a month into my family's visit for my cousin's wedding. I stand a few feet from the garden. My hands cover my mouth and nose. The machli wala sets down a green wicker mat, a round wood cutting board, and three tin pots. Dad and the boys, grins and grimaces on their faces, stand close in a semi-circle around the man. Machli walas ride down the streets every few weeks, ringing their bike bells and shouting, "machli wala, machli!" Even though this is my family's third summer vacation in Karachi, it's the first time on this two-month trip that Ammi let one of them come onto the gated property.

"Is he gonna cut it up right here?" my cousin Humza laughs. "Oh man, that's great."

The machli wala squats over the cutting board. His sandals look like they're made of old tires. He smooths down his moustache and rolls up the brown sleeves of his sand-coloured kurta, a long, tradi-

Chapter 7: Work

tional Pakistani tunic. Most working-class people wear dark brown clothing to hide the dust and sand that settles on them.

The machli wala takes a knife out of a pot.

"Ohh!" the boys shout. The tip of the knife curls upward like an Arabian dagger.

"I can't watch!" my sister Hiba squeals, holding her stomach. She turns and runs into the house.

"It's just fish," Mom says and smiles. "When we were kids, this was the only way we would get fish. Fresh from the sea! It would taste so good."

The machli wala grabs a fish by its tail and slaps it on the wooden board. I wince as he brings down the knife with a thud, chopping off the fish's head. He cuts a slit at the tail of the fish and uses his hands to widen the slit. Bits of white flesh splatter on the orange-tiled driveway as he butchers the fish. A cloud of flies buzzes around the mess. The machli wala, his bare fingers covered in slime, tosses the slices into one of the tin pots.

"This is so gross!" my cousin Maryam says.

"Just wait until you taste it," Mom says.

"Yeah, I'm not eating that," I snort.

The stench is stronger now. It's stronger than the fish section at our local Superstore in Milton. It's worse than the smell of Lake Ontario in July when algae levels are high and the tide carries fish carcasses and seaweed to shore. I wrap my cream scarf around my face. The machli wala continues, unperturbed by the stench and the mid-afternoon heat. He moves swiftly. I wonder if he's been doing this his whole life, or if it's just his day job. I wonder how much he gets paid.

"You should take a video, Halah," Dad says.

"Ew, no!" I shake my head. I don't want to stand looking like a tourist with a clunky DSLR pointed toward the poor guy.

"I'll do it!" Hajir, my youngest sister, says. She runs into the house and comes back a moment later with her digital camera. The machli wala lifts the second fish off the scale.

It's quiet now that the boys went back inside, save for the thump of the knife on the wood and the droning of flies. Hajir points her camera at the man. He squints against the sun, and his sunburnt forehead glistens with sweat. He looks up and smiles at the camera.

"Do this guy, eh," he says in Urdu, holding up the fish towards the camera. Flies bounce off the fish's scales. "Take this guy's photo." The machli wala grins under his moustache and Dad chuckles. Mom explains to the machli wala that she's taking a video.

"Acha," he says. "Oh, okay." He drops the fish onto the board, beams at the camera, and brings down the knife.

The Roti Shop

Selina Africaine

Mrs. Arthur bursts through the bead-curtained doorway. "Ifie, there is someone here to see you."

Mrs. Arthur and her husband own the Nostrand Roti Shop, a small West Indian restaurant in Brooklyn, New York. I work for the Arthurs—illegally since I do not have immigration papers.

I look at Mrs. Arthur's flushed, walnut-coloured face and then at the three rotis baking on the stove. I hold another roti in my hand. I have everything going in a rhythm—the pans at the right temperature, the curries bubbling. I want to meet my quota: fifteen hundred rotis for the day and two huge pots of curry, one beef, the other chicken.

I have a few hours of work before knocking off for the day. I do not want to see anyone. The Arthurs have strict rules against employees bringing personal business into their restaurant. So far, I have complied with all the rules.

I want to tell whoever has come to see me to go away. I need this job. I have my mother, my daughter, my sister and her daughter and myself to take care of. I work illegally. Knowing how much I need this job, I never invite anyone to visit me.

I look apologetically at Mrs. Arthur. I glance at myself in the mirror on the wall near the doorway. White flour covers most of my skin and hair. I look down at my swollen, pained feet. I wear an old pair of Mr. Arthur's shoes. I pray for the hours to pass quickly. I want to get home and soak my feet in hot water and Epsom salts. I cannot go out into the front of the restaurant looking the way I do.

"Girl, whey is this famous roti I hear you a mek?"

I know that baritone voice speaking in Guyanese creole. "Rick!"

A tall, handsome Black man appears in the doorway. He grins mischievously.

"What are you doing here?"

Rick's grin does not seem to belong to the distinguished-looking gentleman before me in a custom-made, three-piece wool suit and spit-polished, black winged-tipped shoes. He looks important and elegant, his well-groomed hair touched with grey at the temples. He looks like an African movie star. Rick is an important man—he runs the Guyana Consulate in New York City.

My ex-boyfriend, Danny, introduced Rick to me, and when Danny and I broke up, Rick and I stayed friends. Rick treats me like a younger sister. He always checks on me to see how I am doing. My face beams when I see Rick come into the kitchen in the back of the Nostrand Roti Shop.

"What the hell?" Rick looks at me standing in the hot, steamy kitchen. The rotis begin to burn. "Get your coat. You are leaving here now!"

"She can't leave now, man." Mrs. Arthur seems just as angry. "Can't you see she is working?"

"Madam, this young woman is a very good friend of mine. She is not a slave and I will not have you treating her as one. I will not stand here and watch you exploit her this way. Do I make myself clear? If you do not let her leave right now, after you pay her whatever money you owe her for her service, I will call the immigration

Chapter 7: Work

service and let you tell them why you are employing an illegal alien. All they will do to her is send her back to Canada."

"Alright, man," Mrs. Arthur says. "I don't want no trouble."

I have never seen Mrs. Arthur move so quick to get my wages. And for once, she has the correct amount. Mrs. Arthur short-changes her employees all the time.

I want to cry. I feel proud knowing that someone cares for me so much. But I also need my job. I stand dumbfounded as I watch the exchange between Rick and Mrs. Arthur.

I get dressed into street clothes, and I think about my family back home in Guyana. I wonder about how I am going to manage now that I don't have a job. I know that the Arthurs rip me off. I make fifteen hundred rotis a day. They sell each roti for two dollars. I work six days a week for one hundred dollars. They make seventeen thousand nine hundred dollars a week from the rotis I make. But I was grateful just to have a job. Compared to what some of my friends earn as illegal immigrants, without any special skills, I was doing better than most.

Rick guides me out to his limousine and holds open the door. I get in. Rick sits beside me.

"Ifie, don't worry girl," he says. "Everything will work out. I am sorry I had to do that, but I could not see you in that situation and let it go. You are my friend. If there is anything I can do for you, you know I will. I just want you to take care of yourself. Look at you, girl. You are so skinny. Look at your feet. I am sure your mother wouldn't want you to get two big feet. You have to learn to say, 'Fuck it!'"

Rick raises my worried face with his hand and looks into my eyes. "Say it. Fuck it! Come on, girl. Say it. Fuck It!"

I look at Rick and smile. I can't do anything about what just happened. I have to look for another job. I have to remember to never again tell Rick where I work. He keeps looking at me with his mischievous grin as he opens the door to let me out.

"Fuck it!" I say.

Rick grabs me into a bear hug. "That's my girl. You will be all right."

He grins again and returns to his limousine. I open the front door leading to my Brooklyn flat. The horn honks, the limousine pulls away, and Rick is gone. I stand at the door for a moment, then run up the stairs.

"Fuck it!" I scream in the quiet flat. "Fuck it!"

It took a while before I found another job. I never again told Rick where I worked. I knew he would never understand that any job I could find would be exploitative. I was, after all, an illegal immigrant, and I had family back home dependent on every penny I sent.

But sometimes I still say, "Fuck it!"

Washroom 1

Eileen Chen

I train for my job at McDonald's.

"When you change garbage, don't use your hands to push it down," Ariel, my trainer, tells me as she shoves down the garbage stopper. It rattles and clunks against the plastic garbage bin. "There might be syringes in there."

We stand in the tiny stall of Washroom 1, consisting of a cracked sink, a toilet that needs cleaning, and a black plastic garbage bin with gunk at the bottom. My eyes follow her actions. I furrow my eyebrows and try to memorize her instructions. I feel out of place in my new blue uniform and the cap that's too tight for my head. Washroom 1 smells like armpit, thanks to the cleaning solution.

~~~

I trudge closer to my McDonald's, wedged between Mario's BBQ and Easy Home on Hurontario Street. Ambulances and police cars at the entrance flash blue and red. I clasp my hands and mumble a small prayer.

I step aside for two EMTs pushing a stretcher. The man on the stretcher wears baggy grey clothes. His eyes, half open, show only the whites. His blue lips tremble. One of his ashy arms dangles over the side of the stretcher. My eyes linger on the red needle marks and his grey nails.

Two policemen follow behind. They hold up a middle-aged man dressed like the man on the stretcher. He slouches and yells over the counter at Vinze, my co-worker, "Why did you open the door for them?" Eyelids heavy, he slurs his words. He coughs and coughs and coughs, and nothing but air comes out. He stumbles, and the police drag him out the door. A string of profanities follows behind them. I hold my breath as they pass. The acrid odour of dried piss is one I'm too familiar with.

I weave between the spectators to the back door. Beef patties sizzle on the grill. I grab the first person I see. "Yo, Vinze, what happened?"

"I don't know. Some crackhead overdosed in the washroom." Vinze washes muffin trays in the sink.

"How many times has it been now?" I pull my hair into a ponytail, hang my hoodie on the hooks by the door, and slip on the visor.

Last week, the police arrested a woman for vandalism in the plaza. She tried to run, but the officer caught her and handcuffed her against the door. Her face left an imprint on the glass. The week before that, a drunk man threw a tantrum because the card reader declined his card. He grabbed the plexiglass separating him and the cashier and smashed it against the wall. I swept the pieces off the floor.

"Why did he yell at you?" I ask Vinze.

"'Cause I opened the washroom for the police."

We walk to the front counter. My shoes stick to the floor. The air smells of burnt bread and spilled coffee. The fryer timer beeps. The fries are ready. The iPad beeps notifications—several Ubereats orders just came in. My shoulders slump as customers flood inside.

"I feel like a celebrity every time I come to work."

"I know, right? Why do all these fat-asses order McDonald's at 11 p.m.?" Vinze punches Uber orders into the machine.

Chapter 7: Work

"You shouldn't be talking," I smirk.

Clarry, the manager, strolls to the front. Rubber gloves cover her new manicure. Her face contorts in disgust.

She interrupts our bickering, "I just got rid of the syringes. One of you go clean the washroom."

I look at Vinze. Vinze looks at me.

"I'll give you twenty," he says.

"You better buy me that new skin on *Valorant*."

I grab some bar towels, a broom, and the cleaning solution that smells like sweat. I stomp towards Washroom 1, ready to salt the fries with my tears for the rest of my eight-hour shift.

Chapter 8: The Interview

Interview someone about something that interests you, and produce an article using material collected in the interview.

Memories

Donald Fitzgerald

"Judith, the *Wheel* is on."

She returns from our kitchen, puts her glass of root beer on her end table, and places my glass of, of what? Ice cubes?

"Where's the drink, Judith?" I ask my housemate and friend.

"Oh, for heaven's sake. I got the bottle out and forgot to pour it. I'll take it back."

She returns with the glass properly filled with Diet Pepsi, stands by my side table, and lowers the glass to my napkin. She cocks her head to the side to see out of one eye. This whole process takes forever. That's always the case with Judith.

Forgetting to put the soft drink in the glass is a minor example of a major medical problem Judith Parsons suffers from short-term memory loss. We watch our favourite TV shows—The *Wheel of Fortune* followed by *Jeopardy*. We spend every evening in front of the television, her on her short couch and me in my plush La-Z-Boy recliner, which she bought me. We have the same tastes in programs.

I conducted this interview during the many three-minute commercials one evening.

Judith came from Whitley Bay on the northeast coast of England in 1952, when she was ten. Her family came over in a cargo boat with staterooms for ten people. They settled in Willowdale in northern Toronto before the subway got that far north. Judith said she had a hard time in school because she was an outsider and her

Chapter 8: The Interview

schoolmates teased her for her accent and clothes. Her early choice of boyfriends proved disastrous.

Things looked up for her after high school. She graduated from secretarial school—not her choice, but her mother's—and then travelled all over Europe and England, then Africa in a Volkswagen Beetle, taking time out to climb Mount Kilimanjaro when it still had snow on top. After a stint with a law firm, she got a job as a secretary for the Federation of Ontario Naturalists (FON), ending up as the editor of their nature magazine. She also had a child, Kent, and enrolled in the University of Toronto in English and Environmental Studies. She took the magazine job home to better manage her studies, her job, and her child.

"Okay, Judith, let's try to get another sound bite on tape during this commercial. You were telling me about what happened at a meeting of some bigwigs at the FON."

"I had a massive brain hemorrhage."

"You had a massive brain hemorrhage?"

"I had what you call a stroke. I was at a business meeting. I was having headaches. I went to see the doctor, and she said I needed a brain scan, and I said, fateful last words, 'I'm too busy on the magazine now. As soon as I put it to bed, I'll go for a scan.'"

"I'd like to buy an A, Alex," a *Wheel of Fortune* contestant asks the game show host. I turn the tape recorder off.

"Am I doing okay, pet?"

"You're doing just fine."

When the next commercial comes on, I say, "We're back. Tell me about the stroke."

"So, I went off to a meeting of government bureaucrats that were helping to fund this particular issue of the magazine, and pounding headache, pounding headache. I felt nauseous. There were about twenty people there, Cabinet Ministers, Deputy Ministers, and the Head of the FON. When we went for lunch, I excused myself to go to the bathroom 'cause I felt violently ill. I collapsed on the floor. The last thing I remember, I'm on the ceiling, looking down on my body, flat on the floor, supine on the floor, people gathering around."

"You had an out-of-body experience?"

"I didn't know that at the time. I was just looking down at these men in black, and I don't remember to this day what the body looked like, just a body, amorphous."

Kent was five years old at the time of his mother's stroke, so he went to live with his father's family. Judith was in a coma for a month when the doctors decided to pull the plug on her breathing machine after filling out the death certificate. But she started to breathe on her own—and lived. After months in the hospital and a year as an out-patient, she returned home and brought Kent home to stay. I came to do some work for her, rebuilding her front steps. And renovation after renovation, I stayed around.

Two side effects persist today from the stroke. She has short-term memory loss, which means she could be introduced to someone in her kitchen, turn around to stir a pot and when she returns to the conversation, she would have to be introduced again. She keeps a daily log, called a Day-Timer, in which she records everything that happens around her. The other side-effect, and the reason she takes so long to put a glass of soft drink down, is that the stroke caused her eyes to go off in different directions. Although surgery has improved that condition, she still sees two images of everything. She usually favours one eye.

Chapter 8: The Interview

"The *Wheel* and *Jeopardy* are over, so let's watch *NCIS*."

The show starts, but Judith says, "I've seen this episode."

"You can't have. It says right in the TV guide that it's new. See the (N) symbol? That means it's never been on before." But that doesn't convince her. She swears she's seen the episode before. She saw a preview of this episode, and she thinks it was the whole episode. She does that all the time. It drives me crazy.

I've learned to stop arguing.

Victoria

Kael Reid

I have to do an interview for a writing class I take at the University of Toronto. A friend of mine, Erin, has a compelling story about her experience growing up with a sibling with severe mental health challenges. I ask Erin if she would share her story with me for my interview. She agrees.

I walk to her one-bedroom apartment one cold, November afternoon. Snow dusts the ground. The crisp air makes my eyes water. When I arrive at Erin's door, she invites me in. She gives me a big hug. Erin is cheerful, but I sense sadness in her. She motions for me to sit down on her faded futon that doubles as a bed. Erin sits in a chair. She sets a pot of peppermint tea on the coffee table between us. The steam curls out of the spout and disappears.

"Thank you for being willing to share your story with me," I say.

Erin looks me in the eyes. "I want people to know what it was like for Victoria."

I nod.

Erin begins. "I'll start with a scene I watched many times."

~~~

Victoria, my older sister, fifteen, is on a weekend pass from London Psychiatric Hospital.

"I don't want to go back there!" Victoria yells. "If you try and make me, I'm calling the police!"

Chapter 8: The Interview

My family lives in an old, stone farmhouse near the rural community of New Hamburg, a small town in southwestern Ontario.

A commotion comes from the kitchen. It's happening again. My chest tightens. I stand silently behind the closed door that separates the kitchen from the living room. I listen, my breath coming in shallow gasps. I hate these weekends, the weekends when Victoria comes home for a couple of days. But then again, I hate the weekends when she's not here.

"Don't start this again, Victoria," Mom says. "You have to go back. You can't stay here." Mom sounds tired.

Every other weekend, the hospital staff lets Victoria come home for a visit. On those weekends, Mom, Dad, my younger brother, Jason, eleven, and I, thirteen, pile into our wood-panelled station wagon and drive from our farm in New Hamburg to London to pick Victoria up and bring her home. It's one hour there and one hour back.

On the way there, Jason and I huddle under a blanket in the backseat and listen to Star Wars stories on cassette tape. We follow along in a little book and look at photos from the movie. A woman's voice narrates the stories. A ping signals it's time to turn the page. The stories take my mind off of why we are driving to London.

I detest going to London Psychiatric Hospital. It's creepy. It feels like its soul has been sucked right out of it. It feels barely alive. My scalp prickles each time I walk through the heavy front doors. I have the feeling that bad things happen here. My heart aches under my ribs as we walk down a long corridor toward the nurse's station. Metal bars cover the windows on stark white walls. Cream-coloured linoleum floors reflect the fluorescent lights from the ceiling. A few light brown vinyl chairs with chrome armrests sit in rows in front of the nurse's station. Small gashes in the vinyl of one chair reveal the white stuffing inside.

A woman shuffles up and down the hallway in her nightgown and slippers, her robe open at the front. The tie drags on the floor as she walks. She mumbles. Another woman, with vacant eyes, paces. Another slumps over in one of the chairs. A small, bubbly pool of drool forms in her lap. Their bodies seem like empty shells. I know the medication makes them this way. That's how places like these keep their patients under control. It's how they keep them from hurting other patients. Or themselves. Seeing them makes me feel hollow. How can people get better in a place like this?

Mom reports to the nurse's station. The rest of us hang back.

"I'm here to pick up my daughter."

She gives them my sister's name. A nurse goes to retrieve Victoria. The nurse's white orthopedic shoes tread silently. A few minutes later, the nurse reappears with Victoria.

"Hi, Vic." Mom hugs her. Victoria smiles a weak smile. She looks wilted. Dad puts his hand on her shoulder and takes the overnight bag from her hands.

The nurse tells my parents that they had put Victoria in solitary confinement. Victoria didn't want to take her medication, and she had a behavioural outburst.

"It was only for a few hours, right Victoria?" The nurse smiles thinly at Victoria. "I'm sure it won't happen again," she chirps. She pats Victoria's back.

I feel sick. How could they lock Victoria in a small room all by herself? She's not a criminal. She's just going through a hard time. She has a mental illness. She's my sister.

Chapter 8: The Interview

We walk out of the hospital into the grey day. Victoria, Jason, and I crowd into the back seat. Today doesn't seem like a good day to fight for a window seat. Dad drives us back to the farm.

I don't remember anything about that weekend except Sunday afternoon when we get ready to take Victoria back to London.

"I don't want to go back there! If you try and make me, I'm calling the police!" she yells.

After a few minutes of listening from behind the door, I open it and go in. What I see feels like a fist to my heart. Victoria yells and cries. She holds the phone in her hand. She shakes. The coiled phone cord bounces up and down as Victoria screams. Dad races over to her, grabs the phone from her hand, and hangs it back on the receiver on the wall. He wraps his big, farmer arms around Victoria's slight body. She struggles, shrieks, and kicks her feet. Mom slips behind them and calls our family doctor. I go over to the window seat, where Jason curls up. I sit down and press myself against him. Jason puts his hand in mine.

Dr. Stephens arrives twenty minutes later. He hurries up to the kitchen door from the driveway with his black leather satchel. Mom lets him in. He sets his satchel on the kitchen table, opens it up, and pulls out a syringe filled with clear fluid. Dad drags Victoria over to the kitchen table. She cries and squirms and screams. Mom and Dad hold her down in a chair. Jason and I watch silently from the window seat.

"No! Nooooo!" Victoria wails. "I don't want to go back! You can't make me! You can't make me!"

Dr. Stephens holds her elbow with one hand and the syringe with the other. He pushes the needle into her shoulder muscle and presses the tiny plunger down with his thumb. The clear liquid disappears into her skin. Victoria's body sags. My parents and Dr. Stephens release their grip. Victoria puts her head down on the table. Her arms dangle at her sides.

The room falls silent. My mom puts her hand on Victoria's back. Victoria whimpers.

Dr. Stephens and my parents step outside onto the walkway in front of the house. They talk. I can't hear what they are saying. Dr. Stephens puts his hand on Mom's shoulder. She covers her face with her hands. I don't know what to do, so I put my arm around Jason.

"I don't want to go back there," Victoria slurs.

I don't remember who takes her back to the hospital.

~~~

Erin exhales and sits back against her chair. I take a deep breath.

"That sounds like such a difficult time for Victoria and for all of you. How," I ask, "is Victoria now?"

"Today, Victoria lives by herself in a one-bedroom apartment in a small town by Lake Ontario. She takes care of herself. She has a social worker who checks in on her regularly and a couple of friends. She takes courses online. She does some volunteer work at the library. She always loved reading. She writes poetry. She doesn't talk to our parents anymore. Hasn't for years. It's better that way for her."

The First Stop

Rachel Smith

Samantha stands across from me in the hallway. We wait for a shelter worker to unlock the office door.

"Today has been a good day," Samantha says. "I got second-stage housing."

Samantha has an unequivocal smile that I instantly mirror back. At twenty, her long legs and long arms move with innocent grace. She has straight blonde hair and almost imperceptible freckles.

"That's amazing!" I say. "What exactly does that mean?"

"Well, I get my own room, and the door can lock. It's one step closer to housing."

Samantha pokes the tip of her slipper into the plush red carpet. The walls are covered in red and gold patterned wallpaper. The second-floor hallway of the shelter looks like a motel but with brighter lights. The shelter worker finally arrives with a six-inch ring of clanking keys.

"Sorry it took so long," she huffs and opens the door.

Two desks, scattered with papers and Post-It Notes, stand on either side of the room. I shut the door and turn one of the office chairs to face Samantha. Her fingers play with the cotton folds of her black sweatpants. She wears a loose-knit yellow sweater and a white and orange striped T-shirt. I remember, despite the public atmosphere, that we are in her home.

She relaxes back in her chair, her long legs leaning to one side.

I met Samantha a few weeks earlier.

The First Stop

Four graduate students and I had set up a meeting at the YWCA to see if there was interest in publishing an arts magazine. Only Samantha showed up the first week. "Is this the meeting for the arts magazine?" she asked. She cradled a notebook and pen. Later, I asked if she was interested in being interviewed, and Samantha said, "Yes."

I turn on the tape recorder.

"Let's start with your name, age, and where we are."

"My name is Samantha O'Conner. I'm twenty years old. Right now, I'm living in a shelter with about forty other women. I've been here since December 3, 2009. I'm living here and going to school, and it's basically because . . . " Samantha stiffens for a moment. "Okay, how am I going to say this?"

There is a brief but intense silence.

"I was brought up in a family with two mentally ill, abusive parents who were addicts. They met in AA, and they beat me and my little brothers. My mom used to beat me with a two-by-four. She called it the Board of Education. She locked me in my room every single night.

"My mom is an evangelical Christian. She is prone to addiction. She went from drugs to alcohol to religion. Now she thinks that everything she does is justified by God. That's why she can beat me with a two-by-four and get away with it. Because it says in the Bible, 'Spare the rod, spoil the child.'"

Samantha speaks quickly but with ease. She says the words as if she has said them many times before. Her young voice carries conviction. "I grew up in Winchester, Ontario, about half an hour outside of Ottawa. I lived with my mom, my dad and my two brothers. We stayed active. We loved school, and we hated going home."

Chapter 8: The Interview

"Did you talk about your home life with your classmates?" I ask. "No! I didn't even realize I was abused until I was eighteen. It was an epiphany. I remember the exact day—where I was, the smells, what I was wearing. I was in a motel room.

"My boyfriend lived in Niagara Falls, and he was coming to visit me for my birthday. I got into a huge fight with my parents. By the time he drove the eight hours to my house, I had already packed my bags and thrown them out the window. We decided to stay in a motel that night. I remember bawling my eyes out and thinking, Look where we are! We are in a motel room in Gananoque! Then I realized, Oh my god, I've been abused.

"I knew my mom hit me and did crazy stuff. We never got along. But I never took in the fact that I was abused. That means something. I realized that all the things I did in my life were because of the abuse. I was on this fast track—partying and not caring about my future. My brain was just shook.

"All the moments in my life flashed before my eyes. 'Look where we are?' I said. 'We are in a motel room in Gananoque!' I said the exact same lines, but this time I was laughing. My perspective totally changed. I thought—I am safe. I am safer than I was before."

"So what did you do after that?"

"I moved in with my boyfriend. I worked on a fruit farm. It was the best summer ever. I got accepted to the University of Guelph-Humber Media Studies program, and we moved to Toronto. I made it through two years of university just fine. We had a cat and all that stuff. When we broke up, he kicked me out of the house.

"I had nowhere to go, so I called my parents. I told them that I needed to come home and work. I took a semester off. I decided to try to fix things with my parents. I thought I couldn't make it without them. I was working three jobs, but I didn't even last a month at home. My mom had one of her bipolar attacks. She's a rapid cycler. She said, 'You're twenty. Get off my property!' She called the cops.

"It's the most frustrating thing in the world, when you're screaming on the inside, but you have to be calm and collected to police officers. If I freaked out, they would have taken my mom's side. So, I had to think about it and be smart about it."

I try to visualize the scene in my mind. It's hard to imagine the radiant, confident girl sitting in front of me in such a situation.

"What was your mother saying about you?" I ask.

"That I'm a dope head! That I'm a crazy, abusive girl! Everything that she is, she switched and said it was me. I ended up in an Ottawa shelter called Naomi's Family Resource Centre. I stayed there from Thanksgiving until the first week of December.

"I needed to go back to school. The shelter workers in Ottawa were like, 'How are we going to get you to Toronto?' They called around to all the different Toronto shelters, and they found a bed there. They called on December 2 and said, 'Alright, we have a bed for you.' I had twenty-four hours to get from Ottawa to Toronto. On December 3, I made it all the way here, all by myself."

"What has it been like being twenty and entering the shelter system?"

"A lot of the women here are in their forties and fifties. I have more time to get my life together and I know I will. I have to learn all these lessons quick and hard."

"What has given you such a positive outlook?"

"Well, I had taken the negative self-pity route. I used to cry myself to sleep every night and think, 'Why me?' I fell into a clinical

Chapter 8: The Interview

depression. Then I realized that my life was more negatively affected the more negatively I thought. It wasn't until I totally flipped things and started living positively that I felt, 'All right, bring it on. Give it to me.'" Samantha laughs.

"You told me about your mom. What was your father like?"

"My dad is a very weak man. I lived with him until I was eighteen, yet I didn't really know him. He's so secretive. He was married before he met my mom. That's when he was an alcoholic, and his ex-wife used to beat him. He's got claw marks on his arms.

"He never did anything when my mom beat me. She was the one who hit us. He never laid a hand on us, but he never did anything to stop it. I don't have anything to say to him."

"Now, who is the most important person in your life?" I ask.

"I am the most important person in my life. I don't have parents who are going to help me. I don't have people telling me I'm doing a good job. So, the only person I do this for is myself. Otherwise, I'll be left behind in the dirt. I won't be able to do all the things I want to do."

Samantha is undeniably ambitious. I wonder how she manages living in the shelter as a full-time student. "What are the challenges of navigating the shelter system?"

"Half the workers are here because they want to help. To the other half, it's just a job. They got into this business because they like the control. They love being able to tell us what to do. Instead of talking to my workers, I talk to the women I live with. Some mature women here who have been through a hell of a lot in their lives. I'm pretty sure I can learn more from them than from someone who went to school and read a bunch of textbooks."

"Have you made any close friends here?"

"Definitely."

"Will you stay in contact?"

"Definitely. I've never really had women role models in my life. I finally know some women who I look up to. Even though they're living here and they're going through some tough times, they keep strong. They are the strongest women who I've ever met in my whole life."

"Do you speak about your experiences of homelessness at school?"

"I'm in this journalism class called Presentation and Persuasion. It's a public speaking course. Every week, we give a speech. The first week I stood in front of my class and said, 'There are over a hundred and fifty thousand homeless people in Canada'—Samantha pauses for effect—'and I am one of them.'

"Their mouths literally dropped! I shared my story and broke the stereotype. I told people that homeless youth are not rebellious, not lazy, and not bums. It just so happens that I was born into a situation beyond my control, and I have to deal with it the best I can. I definitely made a difference in my class. I took my moment." Samantha laughs. "A lot of people mentioned 'bums' and 'homeless people' in their speeches. 'When you see a bum on the street . . . ' I went up there and said, 'I'm homeless.'

"I'm kind of leading a double life. I'm doing really well in my program. I'm always participating in class, doing my work, and I have a social life. So no one would ever expect me to be homeless and living in a shelter. It changed their perspective, and everyone has mad respect for me. They respect me for not being respected." Samantha laughs again. "Does that make any sense?"

Chapter 8: The Interview

I glance down at the list of questions I had typed earlier in the day. Samantha needs little prompting—it's the first time I've looked at the page. One question pops out at me.

"Have you had any experiences in your life that you consider sacred?"

"Definitely," Samantha says. "I've been through so much, but I've done so much. My Opa is a horse whisperer, and I was brought up on a horse farm. My first memories are of horses giving birth. At the age of twelve, I'd get on wild horses and teach them how to ride—break them, that's what they call it. I would just jump on the back of a bucking, wild horse."

Samantha sits straighter and pauses.

"My life is slowly unfolding before my eyes. That's why every night, I go to bed and visualize my dreams. I visualize being a successful journalist. I visualize myself travelling all over the world. I visualize all the things I want because I know they will happen."

Her conviction inspires and troubles me.

"The first twenty years have been lessons, the next twenty will be blessings," Samantha mouths the words as if casting a spell.

I recall my own life. No adequate summation for any person seems possible. But Samantha is convincing, and my uncertainty feels like a betrayal. I look down at the crumpled page of questions.

"Do you have advice to give to other girls or young women who might experience homelessness in the future?"

"Take as much as you can, and don't look down on yourself. Don't look at yourself as homeless. You are on your way to being free from all that baggage from the past. Know that there are people out there willing to help. You are not alone."

Eva Wilkins

Sara Middleton

This story is based on an interview with my grandmother, Eva Wilkens. She talks about her experiences in Germany during the Second World War. It's written from her perspective.

~~~

I grew up in Gross-Jestin in Pomerania, Germany. It was a small town with less than a thousand people. But it was beautiful. We lived two kilometres from the Baltic Sea. Every day my older brother, Johannes, and I cut through the Hindenburg's property, over the meadows, to go swimming in the sea. The white sand stretched for miles.

It was a good life. We never wanted for anything; our bellies were always full. Gross-Jestin had a school, two churches, two stores, a bakery, a drug store—everything we needed.

My family was well off, not in money, but in property. We had the biggest apple orchard for miles and miles. I remember taking a walk with Hindenburg's granddaughter one day, and she admitted to me that she and her sister would steal our apples when we had our backs turned. My mother, Mutti, always told us to keep an eye out. Paul Von Hindenburg was the President of Germany for a time.

He was in opposition to Hitler, and a friend to my father, until Hindenburg died in 1934.

The name "Hitler" wasn't mentioned a lot. If it was, I didn't pay attention to it. I just assumed he was a good guy. I was young. One

Chapter 8: The Interview

Christmas, when I was about ten, I thought it would be a good idea to give my papa a picture of Hitler. When Papa opened my gift, he looked at me and calmly said, "Thank you." He beckoned for me to follow him. I followed Papa into his bedroom. My father placed his finger over his lips. He opened the bottom drawer of his dresser and put the picture of Hitler's face down in the drawer and covered it. Papa shook his head once and never again took the picture out. Not a word was said, in case there were listening ears.

Before the war started, my parents never told me to salute Hitler. So, I never raised my arm when everyone else saluted—until they made us.

Germany went to war when I was thirteen.

Not everyone in Gross-Jestin opposed Hitler. My father's sister and her husband, the Wegners, were Nazis. Wegner was always jealous of my father because he had a bigger home and a better life. But that's just the way it was. When the draft began, my father was supposed to be safe because he was too old and sick. But Wegner and the mayor of our town . . . those Nazis . . . they were supposed to be drafted, but because of their connections, they were able to weasel their way out of it. They pointed their fingers at Papa instead. Wegner and the mayor remained safe, and my sick father was taken to fight a war he didn't believe in.

In the following years, we were able to remain in our home. But there was no school or church. Our days were spent trying to stay safe. Our town eventually became the frontline between the Russians and the Germans. The Germans didn't realize civilians were still there. Every night we heard gunfire and cannons. There would be a bang, and then light, and then a bang, and then light. Like fireworks. I remember the first time I heard real fireworks, years later, in Hamburg. I was so startled; they sounded exactly like the explosions during the war.

One night, my family was huddled in our damp basement on a sack of potatoes. The house shook every few minutes from the cannons and gunfire. We survived the night, and in the morning, Mutti took us to the neighbour's house. She figured we would be safer in numbers. I remember walking across the meadow. I felt a strong urge to get down. As I hit the ground, a bullet flew over my head. I could hear the whistling. I think God saved me that day. I don't know why.

One day when the fighting was bad, the Russians told us to leave and find a safe place. We were sent east where the fighting used to be. We stayed with some soldiers. They fed us, and they were very nice. We went back and forth between there and home for a time. At home, many women and children in town moved into our house for safety. There were about ten women and twenty-five children. We were all scared. Two of my friends were poisoned by their grandmother because she felt death was better than this life.

The soldiers liked to play games with us. One day the Russians told all the males, my brother Johannes included, to go to the market- place. I didn't want him to go. He never returned home.

Then, on March 6, 1945, the Russians came into our town. They told us to pack our things and leave; Gross-Jestin was now Russian territory.

Many died that day. My Russian nanny begged for her life. But they raped and killed her in our home. The soldiers let me say goodbye to her dead body.

We took only what we could carry—food and one blanket each. Our party consisted of me, my mother, my aunt, my little sister,

Chapter 8: The Interview

Ruth, and my little brother, Ernie. We headed west to my mother's old town where her parents still lived. We walked and walked and walked. It felt endless. We slept outside, we slept in a train station, we slept on grass, we slept on tables, we slept in a school, we slept on benches. We never complained. We were too tired to care where we slept.

Wherever we went, we had to beg for food. Many of the places that we passed through lay empty. All the homes had been abandoned. Sometimes we would find an apple tree, and we would eat the apples. It reminded me of home. We wouldn't have eaten them, though, if we thought it was stealing.

We walked for a few weeks. One day a train passed us, and Mutti told us to jump on. We were so exhausted, and the idea of not having to walk was wonderful. So, we jumped on. We thought the train was headed west, but it took us south. We went many miles out of our way.

After almost a month of walking, we made it to the border of the Russian and British zones in central Germany—no-man's-land. There were guards everywhere. Each night I could hear people being shot—by the Russians or the British, I don't know—for trying to cross. We waited for over a month, trying to find a way to cross. Finally, we met a farmer who had property rights on no-man's-land. He was allowed to cross freely. After many arrangements, he agreed to take us across, hidden in his hay wagon. He risked his life for my family.

My mother was scared. If we were found, we would all be killed. I volunteered to go first. I went with my brother Ernie, who was five at the time. We hid in the back of the hay wagon. Halfway through no-man's-land, we transferred to another farmer's wagon, who took us to the other side. There was no time to feel scared.

After we made it across, I took Ernie's hand, and we knocked on doors to find a place to sleep. I didn't worry for my family. Worrying made you do nothing, and I couldn't afford to do nothing. We found a place to stay, and in the morning, the family made us breakfast. Then Ernie and I went to the border where the British were. There was Mutti, walking towards us, safe and unharmed.

After a couple more weeks of walking, we made it to my grandparents' house. Our journey was finally over. When I knocked on the door, there was Johannes. I threw myself at him and hugged him as tightly as I could. We both thought the other was dead. Johannes told us he ran away. He made his own way across Germany and arrived at our grandparents' house only a month before us.

The war ended a couple of months later. It wasn't until 1947 that we found out what happened to my father. We made contact with a German-speaking pastor in France who knew my father. Papa was put in an American-French prisoner-of-war camp in France. He eventually died of starvation. But those kinds of things happened. You had to live through it.

We never made it back to Gross-Jestin, to the sea or to the white sands. We had everything we wanted there . . . at least for a short time.

Alexandra: Bébé de Sucre

Meghna K. Parhar

My friend, Dianne, attends a university on the other side of Toronto. One time, when I visited Dianne at her dorm, I met her friend, Alexandra. When I thought about a person to interview, Alexandra seemed like an interesting possibility. Dianne talked to Alexandra, and we agreed to do the interview in Dianne's dorm.

~~~

The first time I met Alexandra, she held a stack of hundred-dollar-bills. She exuded natural beauty with porcelain skin and green eyes. She was a petite girl, no taller than five-foot-two or -three. Long hazel ringlets fell softly around her face. Five seconds after she introduced herself to me, she talked about her two sugar daddies.

Balancing a Styrofoam takeout-box in one hand and a tall Nestea bottle in the other, Alexandra walked through Dianne's door and smiled. "I'm not late, am I? The line for food was longer than usual." She set down her food on the mini fridge in the corner of Dianne's third-floor dorm room.

"You're right on time, no worries." I grabbed the fat plushie named Tofu from the bottom of the bed and tucked it behind me as a pillow.

"Sit!"

Five first-year girls lounged in Alexandra and Dianne's university residence. Dianne sat at her desk, Emma on the side chair, Sandra on the floor against the wall, myself on one side of the bed, and Alexandra on the other side.

"Can I read the questions while it's recording?" She used her index finger to poke at the screen of my phone. "Yes? Okay, awesome. So, I go by the name Alexandra. The reasoning? A: I don't want them to know my real name, and B: it's much easier to pronounce than my actual name." She chuckled.

"I got into this because . . . I just wanted money!" Her top row of teeth peeked through her thin pink lips. "This just seemed like a fun way to get it, and I honestly don't have any affection toward guys. I want to sleep with them and be done with them, you know? I like the look of them, but not the attachment.

"I met these men on an app called SeekingArrangement. You make a profile with your name, say what you're looking for, and write a little about yourself. Some people just look for someone to hang out with. Other people are obviously looking for more. The guys who pay you usually include their salary, so you know how much they make. Some of them lowball it, some of them highball it. If they're really rich, they'll lie so that girls don't go around telling people they're meeting a billionaire. They message you if they like what they see. I scroll through the messages and reply to those I'm interested in. It's pretty much like Tinder . . . ."

"What about—you said there was a body thing, right?" Dianne asked.

"Oh, yeah, yeah. Some guys want to know your body type, your hair colour, your ethnicity. If they're paying for it, they want what they want." She shrugged her shoulders and cracked the cap of the Nestea bottle in her hand.

Chapter 8: The Interview

"When it comes to filtering, I first like to meet them for coffee or something simple. If I absolutely despise them, I'm like, 'nope, get out!' which has happened before. I wanted a friend who I could do things with. But a lot of these guys are married, so they just want a hookup in a hotel room. I'm not down for that." She clapped her hands together as her eyes got lost in the screen. She tucked a loose tendril of hair behind her ear. Her slender fingers played with the Michael Kors locket that hung from her neck.

"Usually, they tell me their schedule, and I tell them mine. We find a medium, but if I like them, I'll meet up with them more." She used her hands to shoot finger guns in my direction. Dianne, Emma, and Sandra snorted. I motioned for Alexandra to go on.

"What do I do with my sugar daddies? So, above all else, I do have a sexual relationship with them." She chuckled. "One of them, it's like—we don't really have sex. It's mainly just foreplay. The other one, it's everything. We go for dinner, and we've done arcades. I go on trips what else? I've been to the museum, too. We see a lot of movies. They ask me what I want to do, and we do it."

"This seems fun—I want to do it," Sandra chimed in with a smile. Emma rolled her eyes.

"Yeah! And that's the thing. It's never on my dollar, so it's really nice. With guys my age, we go out, and they want to split the bill fifty-fifty, or they'll say, 'you get it this time, I'll get it next time.' Sugar daddies just pay for me, which is great."

"Must be nice," Dianne said.

"I let them know that I don't like public displays of affection around the school area. If they drop me off or pick me up, no getting out of their car and saying hi or bye to me. None of that. Uh-uh." She scrunched her face and shook her head. "In the general public,

I don't really care as much. What's the likelihood I'm going to run into another student?

"Another thing is that I like my personal space. I don't like helicopter people—people constantly texting me, calling me, asking how I'm doing. My school life is most of my life, so I don't like when they interfere with it. Statistics isn't easy, you know?

"I don't like when they're restrictive, which young guys are. Young guys are like, 'oh, you can't talk to this guy, this guy, or this guy, and you can't look at this guy.' But a lot of these guys are fine with me sleeping with other guys."

Dianne raised her hand.

"Would you say there's a big, sugar-baby culture in universities and colleges? I've heard from other people that there are a lot of them."

"There are a lot," Alexandra nodded.

"Everyone's broke at university," Emma said.

"Definitely," I added.

"If you're not paying for tuition, you have to pay for living expenses or going out all the time, which is hella expensive!"

Alexandra used her hands a lot when she spoke. She threw them in the air when she seemed frustrated, and she guided her words with her fingers.

"When I first came to school, my parents told me, 'You have a five hundred dollar budget every month.' In the first month, I blew that like nothing. I called my mom two weeks in and said, 'Oof, that five hundred? Gone.' That was money I made over the summer. Now they manage it for me, so I don't blow it like I did the first time.

"At the moment, I have two sugar daddies. Normally, I meet both of them once or twice a week, depending on their availability.

Chapter 8: The Interview

One of them travels a ton, so it depends. With both, I make close to three thousand dollars every month. That's a lot of money. I started around November, so it adds up. I do save some. But now that I have it, it's hard not to spend. Every weekend I go shopping and blow, what, five hundred? Maybe a thousand?"

"Okay—but what does your mother say?" Sandra piped up.

"That's what I wanna know!" I laughed.

"Oh, I lie like crazy!" Alexandra waved her hand in the air as if it was no big deal. "She knows I get the five hundred a month, so if she ever wants to know where I got that new purse or that new jacket, I just tell her I saved the money, and I lowball the prices. I tell her I buy things second-hand or for five or six hundred less than the price I actually paid, and she believes me."

She paused to sip her Nestea, screwed the cap back on, ran a hand through her curls, and motioned for me to show her the next question.

"I spend most of the money on fashion or food. If I go out, I'll pick up the bill with my friends, and I'll tip, too. I don't really care. But like I said, I do save some of it because I'll have to pay for rent next year.

When it comes to telling people about it—if you tell a girl, she'll say, 'Yes, work it, girl, go get it!' But guys will say, 'You're disgusting,' 'You're a whore,' 'I can't believe you're doing this.' I've definitely gotten some extremely negative comments before. I told this one guy, who I was really close friends with, and he called me a stupid fucking whore bag, so . . . yeah!" The corners of her lips dropped into a scowl.

"You are getting paid to sit there and look pretty . . . there's really no reason why you'd go for just any guy, right?" I asked.

"Oh, definitely. Sometimes we just go out for coffee, and they'll pay for the coffee and for my time. One guy is one-fifty every time I see him, and the other is five hundred. I definitely prefer him because he's often really busy, so even if we only spend an hour or two together, I still get five hundred."

She rearranged her legs to cross over each other on the bed and leaned toward me to scan through my list.

"Safety, safety, safety . . . ," she hummed. "When I first met them, I was definitely worried about safety. It's pretty scary when you go through the meeting process since it sometimes involves them picking you up in the school area. Besides that, once you get to know them, it's very comfortable."

"What are your safety precautions, if you have any?" Emma sat up. We were all curious about that.

"I always tell my closest friend on campus that I'll have her number ready. Dianne usually knows when I'm going out, too. If anything goes down, I'll always be ready to call someone."

"How old are they, if you can say?" Sandra asked.

"The younger one is thirty-nine—"

"The younger one?!" I exclaimed. Sandra burst into giggles. Emma's jaw hung slack.

"The other one is forty, so it's not a huge difference. But the younger one is six-three, Middle Eastern, has facial hair and dark features. He's not out of shape, but not in shape, either. Like a dad bod, but better. The other one is Vietnamese . . . or something? He tells me, but it doesn't stick." The room came alive with more giggles. "He's not too much taller than me. Maybe five-eight? Definitely in shape because he runs marathons. He made his first million at twenty-five.

Chapter 8: The Interview

"The Middle Eastern one dresses very casually—blue jeans, a T-shirt. The other? He's very professional—dress shirts all the time!" She emphasized the last three syllables with hand claps. "I cater my style to who I'm seeing."

With a bounce in her shoulders, she adjusted her sweater. The soft, grey fabric wrapped around her frame like a blanket. She hummed a high-pitched tune as her bright green eyes flicked over the last question on my list.

"Do I consider this a short-term or long-term lifestyle? Well, I have my moments." She pursed her lips and sat up straighter. Her eyes rolled around the room and landed back on the phone. "I'm currently talking to a male who is young and has potential."

"Another sugar daddy?" I raised an eyebrow.

"Nope, an actual guy. He was my Calculus TA." She paused. "See, I used to not be picky with guys. I used to party and always end up going home with someone. Or I'd meet a super cute guy, then find out he just wanted sex. That's why I like sugar daddies—they're more secure. They like long term. They want to take you out for dinner and talk to you. But this younger guy . . . I have this ultimatum since I'm going home in April. He can do whatever he wants over the summer, but if he wants something serious come September, I'll stop with the sugar daddies. But if he doesn't, I'll keep it up. It just makes more sense. The crazy thing is that, if I stayed here for the summer, I'd get paid more with my sugar daddies than I would at home at my regular full-time job.

"If the young guy is into me, into this, I'll get rid of the old men—and take the money loss, which will suck, but . . . " She sighed and shrugged her shoulders, her eyes duller than before. I held back a smile.

"All of this is honestly just a roll-the-dice kind of thing. Maybe I'll get bored of my crazy lifestyle and think eh, I need to move on. Maybe I won't. It's all pretty crazy if you think about it. I definitely didn't see myself doing this, but now that I am, it's fun. This is a way of life. Young guys just can't compare. They can't afford me."

Block 16

Leegun Kim

"Hey, how're you? I'm Lee, Benny's friend. Thank you for taking the time to meet with me."

"No problem man, you can call me K." He speaks with a deep voice, with a slight southern drawl. He slurs his words.

K stands around my height of five-foot-eight. Age twenty-five. He wears a red Derrick Rose Chicago Bulls jersey, with black cargo pants, and a plain black cap. Japanese Irezumi tattoo art covers his arms with flowers, koi fish, and a yurei (a ghost in Japanese folklore) gripping a dagger in its mouth.

Following K's lead, I walk down six steep, concrete steps and enter the rusty red backdoor that leads into his basement apartment. To my surprise, I find a well-lit, newly renovated, wooden-floor basement studio equipped with a small kitchen and a marble-top island with four high chairs surrounding it. Above K's bed hangs a massive painting that depicts a huge US one-hundred-dollar bill. The words "money never sleeps" appear over the painting, in red spray paint. K gestures me over to the black wooden high chairs by the island. We both sit.

"So, I heard you wanted to hear the story of my cell life for some school project?"

"Yeah, that's right, if it's okay with you."

K speaks with ease. His features are soft but his presence intimidates. Most people wouldn't dare to approach K, and he's definitely not someone I would ask for directions.

"Alright, so what'd you wanna know? This won't bite me back, right? I prefer to keep this as lowkey as possible, but I'm willing to share my story, man."

"No no, it won't get you in trouble or anything like that. It's just for my Creative Non-Fiction class."

K places his elbows on the island top and holds his fists with his hands.

"Bet."

I reach over and press the record button. Then, with the click of my pen, he begins.

"I served one year in the Seoul detention centre after being convicted of smuggling drugs into Korea. The street value of the drugs I smuggled was claimed to have been over a million dollars. I got off easy, dawg. I was given a second chance. Frankly speaking, I don't even know how I got out. The crime I committed alone should've been enough to put me away for years, man, years. But, by the grace of God, the judge only hit me with serious probation. I suppose pleading guilty and cooperating with the detectives and prosecutors gave me a good look, plus the fact that I'm young also probably helped. But I'm telling you, man, that shit was a miracle. I couldn't believe it when I was let out.

"But yo, before I get into my experiences inside that shithole, let me enlighten you on why I did all this. Believe it or not cuz, I was a uni student just like you."

My posture stiffens, and my eyes pop open. "Actually . . . ? What made you go from being a student to . . . you know, a drug smuggler?"

"Money, man, money makes the world go round. My family is back in the States facing heavy financial crisis, man, heavy. The fact

Chapter 8: The Interview

that they are undocumented there don't help either. And me? I been living here alone for the past five years. I got nobody here, man. No family, no ties, and no one I knew before I got here. Everything was foreign, dawg. If I don't put food on the table, I can't eat. If I can't pay rent, I'm on the streets. And fuck man, don't even get me started on the school fees. You see, I tried to balance work and school, but that shit ain't no joke, man. It's hard tryna find that balance. The time is just never there. So, I started finding ways to make money quicker, you get me? I made a few chops here and there. Started making connects with him and her, then soon enough the opportunities started growing.

What you gotta keep in mind though is that the risks grow along with it. But see, the thing about us humans is that we all like to think we invincible or some shit, like it'll never happen to me, right? But nah, ain't nobody safe. You can't mistake that. I had to learn that the hard way. So eventually I started climbing and scaling up then, boom. Right when I thought I was about to make it, shit hit the fan."

"Wow that's crazy. When did you serve time? If you don't mind me asking."

"I entered March of 2018 and came out in April of this year. Block 16 was my home."

"I mean you served in a foreign jail. How was that like?"

"I mean I guess I was a lil blessed because I am Korean and I can speak the language, but I have never lived a single year there my whole life. So everything was a shock for me. The culture, the people, and even the shitty food."

"If I may, what was it like in there?"

K leans back on the high chair. His gaze tightens.

"All kinds of fucked, man. That's not a place you wanna land yourself at. I mean, where do I start? Shit, well first they cramp you up in a cell with nothing. No bed, no chairs, no desks, I mean nothing. There's just enough room for five grown men to lie shoulder to shoulder to sleep."

K points towards the kitchen floor. "The cell was prolly smaller than this space right here dawg, imagine that."

I try to picture a cell within the dimensions of the kitchen floor. I just can't see how that was any way for five grown men to live.

"That small? How is that even possible? You guys all just sleep on the floor?"

"Basically, we're given two blankets that you can pull out only during sleep hours: one to lie on and one to cover you. The rest of the time you gotta sit around crossed-legged on the hard floor, and it fucks up the bone on your ankle man. Guys that's been inside for years, those guys don't even got that bone anymore. Them shits are all flat. Not to mention, the guards won't let you lie down so you don't got much choice.

"But yo, lemme tell you, dawg, you'll meet people on all ends of the spectrum there, man. See the thing about being inside is that your stripped down to your bare minimums, and the bare minimum is all you get. Guys get childish in there. They start picking fights over food and shit like leg space. It's crazy man. The summers are too hot and the winters too damn cold. That's why it's hard to sleep at night. You're either suffocating from the heat in that cramped space, or freezing tryna get warm. People go crazy. Most nights you'll hear the screams, man, screams from guys that are on the verge of losing their minds. That shit makes you start questioning your own sanity."

Chapter 8: The Interview

I lose myself in K's story, and all I can say is, "Holy shit."

"Yeah man, but the thing is no matter how shitty things get—be it the food, the people, or the hygiene, somehow you start to adapt. I guess that's what makes us human. You find routine, you start developing tactics, new finesses, new skill sets to survive. It's a dog-eat-dog world in there, so the weak don't last. And when I say the weak, I don't mean physically cause it's a mental thing. Once you've given up, that's it, you become sheep. But the guys that stay attentive, aware, those guys stay alive. I was fortunate enough to have guys like that in my block. I learned a lot from them. They showed me the ropes."

"Wow, this is all so crazy. Okay, I don't wanna hold you much longer so I'll just ask one more question."

I look down at my question flooded paper for a moment. Realizing that I've hardly used the questionnaire, I slide it aside and ask my final question. "Do you have any regrets?"

"Honestly, I don't. Initially, yeah, I regretted the whole thing, but after spending time inside and coming out, I found new gratitude for life itself. I mean I look at myself today and say, yeah this is me. I'm proud of who I am, and I like where I'm at. If it wasn't for my past, maybe I'd be someone else in a different place, you get me? I am who I am because I was able to learn, and overcome my obstacles.

"And if there's one thing I learned in jail it's this. Life is beautiful man, so so beautiful. But no matter how beautiful life is, there will always be darkness in this world. But that darkness is not a means to an end, but rather a doorway to a new beginning. You see, it's because of the darkness you can understand and appreciate what light is. Without that contrast, who's to say what's what, right?

"If you can survive through the darkest of the abyss, then you will never lose the light once you find it, and I believe that. Don't mistake it, though, the dark is a dangerous place. A lot of people lose themselves in there. But yo, if you keep your head up, you'll find the light, man."

Acknowledgements

Thank you to the *Creative Nonfiction* instructors who shared their students' work with us: Professors Geoffrey Bouvier, Claudio Carosi, John Currie, Larissa Ho Fleurette, Kate Maddalena, Robert Price, Gregory Shupak, and Laurel Waterman. We appreciate your expertise and your respect for your students' work.

Laurie Kallis at Life Rattle Press designed and typeset this collection.

Lena Spoke donated the cover art.

Professor Duncan Koerber teaches writing at Brock University and uses peer-based models like the stories in this collection. His appreciation is our "peer review."

The authors whose work appears in this book honour and educate us with your stories. Thank you to the writers.

www.ingramcontent.com/pod-product-compliance
Lightning Source LLC
Chambersburg PA
CBHW021350300426
44114CB00012B/1164